Guideposts to Happiness

Guideposts to Happiness

Prescriptions for a Wonderful Life

Ryuho Okawa

Lantern Books • New York

A Division of Booklight Inc.

2004

Lantern Books

A Division of Booklight Inc.

One Union Square West, Suite 201

New York, NY 10003

Library of Congress Cataloging-in-Publication Data

Okawa, Ryuho, 1956–

[Kofuku-e-no-Douhyou. English]

Guideposts to happiness : prescriptions for a wonderful life / Ryuho Okawa.

p. cm.

ISBN 1-59056-056-6 (alk. paper)

1. Kofuku no Kagaku (Organization)—Doctrines. I. Title.

BP605.K55O3225 2003

299'.93—dc22

2003022563

printed on 100% post-consumer waste paper, chlorine-free

Table of Contents

Preface

This book consists of two parts. Part One includes a lecture I gave at a seminar entitled "Guideposts to Happiness" in 1989, for members of the Institute for Research in Human Happiness which I founded. Chapters Two and Three are additional materials on pride and arrogance, and the self-tormenting mentality, which were not discussed in detail at that lecture.

There is an almost infinite variety of subjects related to the theme "guideposts to happiness." When discussing a topic, unless I am able to explain it from different angles and give concrete examples, readers will not understand fully what I say nor will they consider these issues to be problems that concern them directly. This book will bring you great joy as it describes specific ways of thinking and attitudes that hold the human spirit back on the path to happiness.

Part Two is a collection of writings that were published as Monthly Messages for our Institute between January and June 1989. These cover a variety of subjects, and I have outlined a number of important ways of thinking, linking them to the seasons. I believe that this book will serve as a valuable reference and be used as a textbook to study ways of achieving true happiness.

Ryuho Okawa
President
The Institute for Research in Human Happiness

PART ONE

Chapter One

Guideposts to Happiness

1. A Great Need for Doctors of the Soul

For this chapter I have chosen the title, "Guideposts to Happiness." As the founder of the Institute for Research in Human Happiness, I always wish that I could listen to the worries of each member personally and provide clear-cut solutions, giving appropriate advice wherever needed. But the reality is that it is impossible for me to do this because the number of members has grown to be so large. For this reason, I have decided to publish books about attaining happiness in the hope that you will use them as guides and in them find solutions to your own problems. I would like you to use these as reference books; they give model answers to everyday problems. Providing these books is an expedient way of guiding large numbers of people.

However, I am well aware that those who have worries want to talk to someone personally to find answers that apply to their own unique situation. Actually, it is impossible to offer advice that applies to everyone, and it is unrealistic to expect a single theory to solve all difficulties. This is why there is a great need for "doctors of the soul" who can give advice to individuals.

Today, medical doctors are well-respected. Many people wish to get the qualifications to practice medicine and, as a result, there are many doctors trained to treat the physical body. However, there is an even greater need for doctors who are able to treat mental and spiritual problems. Looking around, I see so many people suffering from illnesses of the soul that I feel there is a pressing need for large numbers of doctors able to treat these illnesses.

If you have a toothache or any other health problem, you can always find a doctor or dentist to consult who can treat you. Overall, the modern medical system is quite adequate. In contrast, for spiritual problems, people have no idea of where to go or what kind of consultation to look for. Even if they consult someone there is no guarantee that they will receive the right answers. This is one of the reasons I have established the Institute for Research in Human Happiness. It is my wish to produce many qualified doctors of the soul who can treat spiritual problems. With this aim, the Institute offers seminars to educate members so they can acquire knowledge and develop the ability to give people advice about their worries. It is my sincere wish, with the help of these doctors, to cure the illnesses of the soul of people all over the world.

Some people may find the study requirements of the Institute rather demanding, but if you think about how difficult it is to become a medical doctor, you will understand why this is so. We expect someone who wishes to become a doctor to study very hard, otherwise we cannot rely on that person for medical consultations, nor do we feel confident when being treated by them. I am sure I am not the only one who wishes that every would-be doctor could pass a national examination with full marks. I wish every doctor were competent enough to diagnose all sorts of illnesses accurately and treat them correctly. Indeed, a doctor can never be too competent.

The same can be said of doctors of the soul. I would like doctors of the soul to excel in finding solutions to the different problems people have. My books are full of examples of spiritual illnesses and their

so I want them to study as many of these
possible and give advice that is appropriate to
lea.   ople to happiness. There will be no limits to the
demand for their skills. However hard they study and
however deep their understanding, it can never be too
much.

2. Happiness and Unhappiness

Now, let us look at happiness more deeply from a
practical point of view. The fact that our organization
is named the Institute for Research in Human
Happiness shows how much emphasis we place on
happiness. We always have to remind ourselves that
all our activities at the Institute are for the realization
of happiness on Earth.

What does the term "happiness" mean to you?
What kinds of situations represent a state of happiness
and what kind represent a state of unhappiness? I
would say that people who are happy are those whose
minds are filled with pictures that are pleasant to them.
On the other hand, the minds of those who live in a
state of unhappiness are full of unpleasant images.
This is the key when discussing happiness and unhappiness. When looking at happiness and unhappiness,
we have to grasp the true nature of what we usually
think of as worries.

When you worry, the images in your mind are far from any ideal. If you constantly paint pictures in your mind of what you do not want, it reveals that you are in a state of anxiety, and the continuation of this state is known as unhappiness. In short, an unhappy person always has negative pictures on his or her mental canvas, whereas a happy person creates positive images.

When I chose the title "Guideposts to Happiness," I did not intend to outline any grand theories about the rules governing this vast universe. I would like to explain the simple truth about life, the most fundamental exploration for every individual. There are thousands of ways to explain the nature of the mind, but the simplest is to say that everyone has a blank mental canvas, and draws certain pictures on this canvas every day. It is the pictures that you draw on your mental canvas that determine whether you are happy or unhappy.

Consequently, it is necessary to examine objectively what kind of pictures you are drawing. Look at the picture you are drawing now. If you are always focusing on the negative and complaining, your mental pictures are far from beautiful. Then ask yourself these questions: Why do I draw such unpleasant pictures? Why are my sketches so misshapen? Why do I use gray so often? Although there are a lot of beautiful, bright colors, why do I like to use gray and black, such drab colors?

There are two major reasons for drawing such negative pictures. One is disappointment as a result of past failures. If you had a dream that ended in failure, the feeling of loss may persist for quite some time. Such setbacks can lead to discouragement and some people do not easily recover; they continue to have negative mental tendencies. Another major reason for dwelling on dark mental pictures is an inferiority complex, which may or may not be connected to past failure. Feelings of inferiority lead to self-hatred and loss of confidence, and these negative feelings will cause you to choose somber colors for your mental pictures. If this is the case, you need to know why these negative thoughts come into your mind.

3. What to Do about a Sense of Failure

To begin with, let us look at the disappointment resulting from failure. Why do some incidents in your life disappoint you? It sometimes happens that although you have a certain image of yourself and expect others to treat you in a certain way, the reality is somewhat different. Then you become unable to bear the gap between your self-image and the reality of how you are treated. I would not say that you should always deny such feelings. Sometimes people do treat you unreasonably, which may be upsetting and cause you to feel disappointed. However, even if you are put in a difficult position as the result of someone else's misjudgment, if you continue to feel disappointed, this will become your reality. As long as you remain trapped by disappointment, you can never free yourself from unhappiness.

To cope with disappointment, there are three attitudes you can adopt. Firstly, calmly accept reality as it is and remain undisturbed. Secondly, never be discouraged by failure and tackle a problem again and again. Thirdly, try to find a solution from a completely new angle. Revolutionize your perspective and discover a third way to solve the problem. I would like to discuss each of these three attitudes one at a time.

1) Calmly accept reality as it is and remain undisturbed
This attitude may seem passive, but it is a key to overcoming hardships in life. Actually, what you consider to be failure or disappointment is often not as serious as you imagine. You may take "failure" very seriously, focusing too much on yourself, as if the whole universe revolved around you.

Even if you feel that you cannot accept an experience and your ego has been wounded, to everyone else your situation may seem quite unremarkable. Nevertheless, you play the role of the tragic hero or heroine, struggling in agony, and as you continue to behave like this, your suffering increases further. It is you alone who aggravate your own suffering. Unfortunately, people often do this.

In this sort of a situation, you should view yourself objectively and unemotionally, as if from a distance. Imagine how many people there are in the world who are in a similar situation, and you will realize that your problem is not as serious as you thought. It is your imagination that has made the situation seem so critical. This may appear to be a passive approach, but it is a very useful attitude to adopt in many situations in life.

In this world, there are many things you cannot control. You are not the only one who has experienced this: I, too, have exactly the same problem. For example, I cannot make people think in the way I would like. I could see this as a problem and feel frustrated, but I would rather ask myself, "How realistic is it to try to control things?" and then adopt a realistic attitude. This is not at all a passive way of looking at a situation. Often you can solve anxieties simply by being unattached to a particular issue. If you look at people who are always worried, you will find that they are too sensitive. They take small issues very seriously, and constantly complain about the same things. These sorts of people usually become too attached to things and situations, in other words, they are obsessive. They hold on too tightly, and this attitude itself creates worries. Nevertheless, they blame others for their unhappiness and in this attitude lies their biggest mistake.

I often say that if a number of people were placed in the same situation, each person would think and behave in a different way. What I really want to say is that even if a problem you are facing seems very serious and unique to you, other people will see it in a different way. For example, if I were in your place, or if an angel of light were dealing with the same problem you face, the outcome would be different, so it is wrong to see a problem or an unhappy state of mind as the natural outcome of a particular situation. Your own character and mental tendencies are the determining factor.

If you are struggling to get rid of your problems, here is a useful piece of advice: Worries are something you create—so as soon as you stop creating them, they will disappear automatically. Faced with failure, one person may suffer disappointment for ten years while another may forget about it within a day or two. Who is responsible for this suffering? Suppose someone has spoken harshly to you and you feel deeply wounded. Who is to blame if you are in pain for the next ten years? Does the responsibility lie with the person who spoke harshly or with you who were on the receiving end of those words? Think about the answer. Actually, the cause of your misery may be someone's words, but it is only you who are choosing to take them so seriously. Had you wanted to, you could have forgotten this unpleasant incident.

I would like you to remember that it is you yourself who create the problems. So, before you complain about the negative things that happen, first analyze your own character. Then if you find you have a tendency to worry about small things, thinking about the same issue over and over again, resolve to be more lighthearted and not to fuss over the small things. Your determination is the first step to overcoming the tendency to worry and, if you resolve to develop a different character, you will gradually achieve this. You will never achieve happiness if, as a result of one experience of failure, you develop a persecution complex and become obsessed with the idea that everyone is speaking ill of you. You need to be more lighthearted.

There are two attitudes necessary to be more lighthearted. One is to learn the lessons from a setback, and the other is to see any setback as an opportunity to change things for the better. Revolutionize your perspective and try to think of a setback as an opportunity for you to achieve greater success. Instead of simply being overwhelmed by failure, or thinking that it is the end of the world, take advantage of the next opportunity. Otherwise, you will perceive even the next situation as part of a continuing series of setbacks and fail to notice the opportunity. Once you recover from a setback, you will find it easy to understand why it happened, but in the middle of it, it is not easy to see the whole picture. However, you can still try to learn the lessons from a failure, and search for the path of continuing development.

Being lighthearted has yet another meaning, which is being able to see things objectively from a higher perspective. For example, problems that seem so difficult to adolescents may seem insignificant to older people because they have been through the same sort of experiences several decades before. Quite often, the problems of youth can easily be solved with the wisdom of older people. In the same way, try to look at a problem and analyze the possible outcomes from a higher perspective, then you will be able to see the whole picture clearly and understand what is really happening to you. Usually problems are not as serious as you imagine, so please make an effort to adopt this approach. If you do, you will be able to avoid becoming trapped by details.

2) Never be discouraged by failure—tackle a problem again and again
The second attitude for coping with disappointment is to take up a challenge again and again. Never give up. Perseverance allows the possibility that a new path will open up. If you use your setback as an opportunity to make more effort, you may achieve greater success next time. This attitude is praiseworthy; if you give up too easily, your life will not bear fruit. If you find something that is worth doing and decide to pursue a particular path, you should go as far as you are able and, in the process, you will grow spiritually. It is important to see past failure, using it as a springboard from which you can jump higher.

It is possible that failure may leave a wound in your heart. In this case, I would recommend that you focus on achieving further success, rather than struggling to heal the wound. Do not focus on failure in the same way as you would focus on an ink stain on a blank canvas; instead aim to paint beautiful colors around the blotch. Nothing can be done to reverse past failure, so it is much better to learn the lesson from it and aim for greater success in the future. It is important not to punish yourself forever for past failures.

3) Try to find a solution from a completely new angle
The third attitude I recommend for coping with disappointment is to find an unexpected path leading in a new direction; find a completely new solution. I sometimes talk about finding "the pin," or the ultimate root of a problem.

The French philosopher, Alain (1868–1951), recounted the episode of a baby who would not stop crying no matter what its mother did, no matter whether she gave it milk, or raised or lowered the temperature of the room. Finally, the mother sent for a doctor who diagnosed nothing wrong with the baby. Eventually it was discovered that the baby was crying because there was a tiny pin in its sweater that was pricking. Similarly, when you look at a problem from a completely new angle, often you can find an unexpected way out. The more new ways of seeing a situation that you can discover, the more easily you will find the "pin," a third way of solving a problem.

Often we become slaves to habit without even realizing it. If we keep on failing, we tend to become trapped by a sense of failure. As a result, we quickly fall into the same pattern of failure, no matter what the situation we are placed in. At these times, it is essential to try to find completely different options for solving a problem. Coping with difficulties in this way can be called "diversification." When facing worries, it is important always to be on the lookout for ways of increasing the possibilities in life.

These days, this strategy is used in both professional and amateur baseball. In the old days, one strong pitcher often played right through for the whole game. However, today there are usually two or more pitchers sitting on a bench, waiting to play when needed. Having one very strong pitcher who continues to pitch to the end of the game and defeats the opposing team is the ideal, but this does not always happen, so different pitchers are held in reserve in case they are needed. Because he has readied several alternative pitchers, if the team plays poorly in the beginning, the coach is able to take action. This is how coaches reduce the risk of losing.

Similarly in life you have to take these sorts of precautions against possible failure. Prepare two or more options in advance, and refine your problem-solving skills so that you can get through any difficulty. In the same way that even professional pitchers cannot always win the game, you cannot always fulfill your dreams because along the way there are often obstacles awaiting. It is good to have emergency measures prepared beforehand to cope with this.

One of the reasons failure brings with it a deep sense of disappointment is that people often have just one aim in life. It is fine to fix on a goal and strive to achieve success. But if you think too much about one particular goal, and see it as the only way to make your dreams come true, your determination becomes attachment. As a result, even small failures may result in serious disappointment. This is no different from limiting yourself to just one profession in the early stages of your life. You may have forgotten the broader perspective—that you have far greater potential than you may think. While struggling to solve a problem, it is important always to make room for other possibilities. This serves as one of the main ways of avoiding disappointment.

4. What to Do about an Inferiority Complex
I talked about disappointment and now I would like to discuss a problem that often arises out of experiencing failure—an inferiority complex. A sense of inferiority is a deep-rooted insecurity and often the direct cause is past failure.

When I analyzed people's worries, I found that most of them arose out of an inferiority complex. No one is without an inferiority complex of some sort. Since everyone has one, you should think about how yours came into existence. If you are creating worries because of an inferiority complex, you need to analyze this and find ways of overcoming it.

There are many different ways to overcome a sense of inferiority but again, the most basic way is to use it as a springboard. This method is quite easy to put into practice, and you may often come across people who have managed to get through their difficulties this way. However, the problem is that even if you achieve success, you will not feel completely satisfied.

People who want to show off usually have an inferiority complex and use it as a driving force in achieving their aims. But no matter how much they show off, these sorts of people are never completely satisfied because they are well aware of their own sense of inferiority. Even people who appear frequently on television suffer inferiority complexes. Even some of those who are past middle age still use their insecurity as a springboard, becoming unnaturally active and trying hard to make a name for themselves, in an effort to overcome their insecurity. However, as long as they behave like this, their inferiority complex will not diminish.

It may be the case that the larger the inferiority complex, the greater the success a person achieves by using it as a springboard, but such success only causes others to feel sorry for that person because their inferiority complex is so obvious. There is a well-known Japanese critic who is very active writing and lecturing, and who often appears on TV. Personally I have great respect for his energy and ability, but at a glance it is obvious that he has a powerful inferiority complex. One of the reasons for this complex is his appearance—it seems he does not have any confidence in the way he looks. Another reason is that he quickly becomes bored with things; he is easily distracted and jumps from one thing to the next, unable to concentrate for long on any one thing. To compensate for his inferiority complex, he is all the more active in many areas and, as a result, is considered quite successful in the world. Nevertheless, I can see clearly that he is not satisfied with himself.

To take another example, there is a famous scholar who is recognized as one of Japan's foremost opinion leaders, and whom I respect profoundly. Through hard work he has acquired a very insightful perspective on history, which I find enlightening in many ways. However, even someone as outstanding as he seems to have a sense of inferiority. Reading his works carefully, I feel that he has a powerful sense of inferiority simply because the university he graduated from was not ranked very highly in Japan at that time, just after the Second World War. Although he has a very high level of intelligence, much higher than graduates of the top universities, he nevertheless appears to be ill at ease about his educational background.

His inferiority complex has long been the driving force behind his wide-ranging work, which has brought him great success. Despite this, I feel he is not completely satisfied, and in this respect I feel a little sorry for him. I would like to give him some words of encouragement, and tell him he should be more confident because he is better than he thinks. Unfortunately, his sense of inferiority seems to have been something of an obstacle for him.

Recently I enjoyed reading a series of autobiographical articles in the newspaper by Shusaku Endo (1923–1996), a renowned Japanese novelist. He was always humorous and wrote a lot about his past failures. He is actually someone who became successful by using his sense of inferiority as a springboard, and the fact that he could write about his failures indicates that he gained great self-confidence.

When he was young, he used to feel inferior to his brother but through his marvelous literary achievements he managed to overcome his negativity. He openly wrote humorous stories about past failures. I am impressed to see that he succeeded in overcoming his inferiority complex, transforming it into the energy to produce amusing stories. Being able to talk about past failures without embarrassment and using them to evoke humor is proof that an inferiority complex has gone. Our aim should be to achieve this sort of attitude.

You may have something you want to keep secret from others, or that you feel ashamed of. Think how you could talk about that secret openly and humorously. In fact, a sense of success will offset past failure, negative feelings about yourself, or dissatisfaction at your lack of ability. Experiencing a success that gives you confidence will undoubtedly help you overcome an inferiority complex, and you will then be able to talk about it with humor. You will be able to tell others about past failure in the form of funny stories and your experiences will encourage others who are worried about their own inferiority complex.

As the prescription for an inferiority complex, I would advise you to use it as a springboard for walking the path to success. However, you should not stop here. You need to proceed to the next stage, where you can feel confident about your success. First, you need to be able to acknowledge your success yourself, then it is necessary that others recognize it. The acknowledgment of others will give you greater inner peace. What do you need to do next? You should never try to vent your own suffering by forcing others to experience the same pain that you have suffered as a result of your inferiority complex. Do not increase their pain by insisting they need to experience hardship, or by sticking a knife into the wound in someone's heart. Instead, share your painful experiences with others in a humorous manner so that you can give comfort and show them a way out. You need to reach a level where you can do this.

I feel sorry for people who are still trying to attract attention to themselves in middle age by boasting about past achievements. These people need to use the failures and disappointments they have experienced to provide wisdom to help young people solve problems. As they get older, people tend to like to talk proudly of past successes; instead, they need to talk about past failures in a way that eases the anxieties of others.

If you are middle aged, instead of trying to cover up past failures and boasting about current successes, open your heart to young people and, to encourage them, tell humorous tales of your youthful failures. Do not pretend to be someone who has never experienced failure; you must have had many useful experiences, so make it a goal to become the sort of person who is willing to use these.

If you find yourself able to talk openly about past failure, it means you are already successful. As long as you are keeping up appearances, it proves that you are not completely happy with yourself. When you are satisfied with yourself, you will be able to tell others quite easily about an inferiority complex. Afterwards, if you regret having told your secret and become so distressed that you are unable to sleep, your wound has not yet healed. It is admirable to be able to give advice to others who worry, drawing freely and lightheartedly on actual experiences of failure. I would like you to aim to reach this point.

Although it is not really commendable, it is human nature to feel relieved and comfortable to know that other people have experienced failure too. If you have made your way in the world, you should sometimes use past episodes to encourage those who are worried, and give them hope. This will have the effect of loosening some of the tension in this world. You should not just point out others' shortcomings; you should also give advice that is appropriate, based on past failure, so that they can solve their own problems. A really successful person can give useful advice in this way.

Generally speaking, anxiety arises from the fact that people think their troubles are unique. When you become aware that you are not the only one suffering a particular problem, it will cut your worry in half. When you discover that the same problem can befall others, you can begin to find solutions by examining what has happened in their case. You can even benefit from anxiety because it is an opportunity to study what is common to all worry, and to understand human nature. By studying the different sorts of worries that people have, you will come to know yourself better and acquire a deeper insight into human nature.

5. Abandon the Tendency to Love Unhappiness

Having talked about different ways to overcome worries, I can summarize my advice in just one sentence: Choose to think in a way that will truly benefit you. When you are in the midst of worry, your heart is usually torn apart by two, three, or more different choices and you begin to lose control. In this instance, ask yourself what kind of thinking will benefit you most and you will know the answer.

Take, for example, an examination. Naturally, some people pass and others fail; interestingly, however, even among those who have passed some are furious simply because their marks were not as high as they expected. They believe they have the potential to score high marks, so even if they have passed, they cannot accept the results on account of their pride. On the other hand, others are really delighted to have passed and feel grateful, despite the fact that their score was barely a pass mark. These are two different attitudes.

Think deeply about which one will bring you greater happiness. In this example, the second attitude is obviously more beneficial. To extend this way of thinking, the second type of person may well feel thankful for their low marks because it is a chance for them to realize with humility that they must start again and continue to study harder. There are many different ways of looking at exam results and you need to consider which way of thinking will make you happy.

If you choose a way of thinking that makes you feel unhappy, you cannot blame anyone except yourself. You will have to suffer as a result of your own choices. Unfortunately, this is often the case. When faced with a situation that may worry you, think seriously and thoroughly about all the possible options. If you find two, three, or more possible ways of thinking, judge which one will bring you the greatest happiness.

You may find yourself in the midst of different worries, but do you truly want to be happy? This is the vital question. If you want to be happy, first make a resolution to be happy. Then you will naturally know what you should do to achieve this. However, most people do not truly know whether they want to be happy. Looking at those who often ask others for advice about their problems, I suspect that, deep in their hearts, some people even love unhappiness and embrace it. Many people try to find explanations for their unhappiness by attributing it to karma or destiny. It is also human nature to justify worries. People find many different justifications; some even insist that because Jesus Christ suffered it is natural that they too should suffer.

What is important firstly is to ask yourself which way of thinking will benefit you most, and whether you really want to be happy. Unfortunately, some people have a tendency always to choose the option that will make them unhappy, and there is no way to help them. They even interpret advice from others in a negative way. God always gives you a helping hand, but if you choose unhappiness and fall on your own, even God cannot help you because this is within the range of human free will. So it is important that first of all, you are determined to choose happiness.

It may be hard to believe, but there are actually people who love being unhappy, people who want to stay in the tepid waters of unhappiness. They believe that if their unhappiness is taken away, they will shiver with cold, as if their coat had been removed, so they prefer to hold onto it rather than try to take it off. They love and embrace unhappiness with great care, because they believe that as long as they have one sort of unhappiness, a more severe unhappiness will not befall them.

Perhaps it is not very easy to check and see for yourself whether you have this tendency to love unhappiness, so look at others and watch them carefully. See if they love and embrace unhappiness, then look back at yourself once again and compare yourself with those people. If you find similar tendencies in yourself, you have to understand that you alone are choosing to be unhappy; you cannot blame God or your guardian spirit for your unhappiness. Only after you come to realize this will you be ready to take off the coat of unhappiness.

Do you understand what it means to love unhappiness? Some people become depressed because they do not realize how blessed they actually are. A lack of gratitude is one of the checkpoints for the tendency to love unhappiness. Typically, people who love unhappiness are those who are actually suffering either a sense of disappointment resulting from failure or an inferiority complex. Basically, they think only of themselves. They are anxious to be loved; in other words, they are obsessed with a love that "takes." If you get closer to them, you will feel as if you are being deprived of something, your energy or your vigor. As a result, people choose to keep their distance from this type of person.

If you discover the tendency to love unhappiness in yourself, there are basically two ways to overcome it. The first way is to choose to be someone who gives love. If you love being unhappy, you are actually depriving others of love, so make an effort to give love to others and enjoy other people's happiness as if it were your own. People who love unhappiness usually think that other people's happiness is the cause of their suffering and that it makes them feel miserable. However, they should start by giving to others. Only when they direct their minds to pay more attention to others will they find that their own worries disappear.

Although similar to the first, another way to change a tendency to love unhappiness is to give others your blessing. If you do not bless others, you will never escape from the state of unhappiness. When you see someone who is happy, it is important to accept that fact because the moment you appreciate others' happiness, you are already beginning to approach the state of happiness that person embodies.

If you can admire others when you acknowledge their good points, then you are already beginning to abandon the tendency to love unhappiness. Being able to acknowledge that someone is wonderful means you wish to be like that person, and you cannot hold onto your misery any longer. If you feel jealous or wish that person harm, you will never be happy. In the news media, I often see examples of people who do this. They have a tendency to find fault with those who are successful. This is not the way to happiness. Instead, when they see a wonderful quality in someone, they should aspire to be like that person, and encourage others as well, otherwise they will never be able to move out of the depths of unhappiness.

To close this chapter, let me summarize how to recover from misery and become truly happy. First, try to give love to others; secondly, give your blessing to those who are happy. These attitudes are essential if you are to rise out of unhappiness and become truly happy. I hope that you will be able to solve your own problems, using this message as your guide.

Chapter Two

Pride and Arrogance

1. The Difference between Pride and Arrogance

In this chapter, I would like to discuss pride and arrogance, both of which are causes of annoyance in today's society. Although there are certain commonly accepted definitions of both pride and arrogance, until now there have not been clear definitions of these concepts in the light of Truth. For this reason I would like to lay pride and arrogance on the cutting board to analyze and dissect them.

Let us start by examining whether pride and arrogance are the same. These two concepts overlap and are sometimes used interchangeably to convey the same meaning. But while the word "arrogance" usually has negative connotations, the word "pride" has both positive and negative meanings, depending on the

n. For example, people who are talented and successful are usually proud, and to be proud is not necessarily wrong. However, if these people demand that others hold them in high regard and others disapprove of their pride they will be regarded as arrogant.

To be proud of your social status, your income, your job, or your responsibilities is fine as long as the pride remains within appropriate bounds. When your desires are being realized, naturally you will feel a sense of fulfillment and satisfaction. However, if you develop an unduly high opinion of yourself, pride quickly leads to arrogance and, as a result, you and also others will be drawn into suffering.

2. Three Checkpoints for Arrogance

The question is whether or not pride is justified. To check on this, you need to see yourself objectively, as practiced in Right View, the first step of the Noble Eightfold Path.[1]

To determine whether or not your pride has turned to arrogance, you need to measure yourself against three yardsticks. Firstly, check whether or not you see yourself rightly, in an objective way. Secondly, calmly

---

1. Refer to *The Laws of the Sun* (Lantern Books, 2001), *The Golden Laws* (Lantern Books, 2002) and *The Essence of Buddha* (Time Warner Books, 2002) by Ryuho Okawa.

examine how others see you, and thirdly, check and see how you evaluate others.

Let us examine the first checkpoint. How do you evaluate yourself? If you have an unduly high opinion of yourself, it means you are too proud and are likely to be arrogant. If you examine yourself, you can easily understand this.

Secondly, examine how others see you. Here there are two extremes. If you are not content with others' opinions of you and feel that their evaluations are unreasonably low you will tend to assert yourself aggressively in an effort to alter their perceptions of you. At the other extreme, if people's assessments of you are too high, you may mistake their appraisals for reality and develop a false sense of pride, becoming arrogant in the eyes of others.

Thirdly, examine the way you see others. If you cannot see other people's good points or if you look down on others, you are in danger of becoming arrogant and egocentric, and you will gradually develop a strong desire to assert yourself. If you hold others in low regard and rate yourself too highly in relation to them, pride becomes excessive.

If, on the other hand, you overestimate others, you will be in danger of developing feelings of inferiority. If you could accept your feelings of inferiority calmly and objectively, this would not cause any harm; however, if you nurse grudges toward others and become hostile, your actions will arise out of an attempt to offset these feelings. As a result, others will find your speech and actions aggressive and out of character, and so they will label you arrogant.

The desire to assert oneself involves a serious struggle to acquire an assessment of the self that is appropriate. Throughout life, we are continually endeavoring, or in a sense struggling, to assess our own worth. This is why pride and arrogance are fundamental to all human beings, and we cannot easily escape them.

3. What Lies behind Arrogance

I would not state flatly that pride, or the desire to assert oneself that is based on pride, is wrong in itself. Look at Mother Nature. You could say that all animals and plants have a desire to assert themselves. Fish, birds, and flowers also seem to have a desire to stand out. Looking at the different colors of flowers, they seem to compete with one another to display their beauty. Animals also seem to be competing to prove their strength.

Observing nature, I feel that at the root of the desire to assert the self are the principles of advancement and evolution, and a desire to grow. The desire to progress constantly, to expand further and develop oneself without limits—these are at the root of the desire to assert the self.

Seen from this perspective, you will understand why people dislike arrogance and why you feel embarrassed if you find you have been arrogant. From the point of view of the individual, the desire to fulfill one's potential and the desire for limitless growth are praiseworthy. These desires are in harmony with the laws of the universe. But when you assert yourself too much and become arrogant, negative feelings arise between you and others, because in the same way that you wish to grow without limits, others also have the goal of infinite development.

Imagine the growth of trees. When a tree grows tall, it blocks the sunlight from the trees and plants below and their growth is impeded. Much the same happens with people. Each person wants to grow, but if one person grows too tall, that person will cast a shadow over the others, blocking their sunlight. This is the conflict between progress and harmony.

Progress and harmony are two factors that can be likened to the vertical and the horizontal axis on a graph. Progress is vertical, rising to infinite heights, while harmony is horizontal and aims to coordinate

th others. At first glance, these two factors
o be in conflict with one another. However,
God s w..l is to encourage the whole universe to
develop magnificently through balancing these contra-
dictory factors.

This is why those who assert themselves too
strongly are always on the receiving end of criticism
and jealousy. Having grown too tall, they have become
arrogant, and their attitudes that put others in the shade
arouse rebellion.

4. How to Overcome Arrogance

Now you have probably understood why arrogance is
considered a problem. The reason is it engenders an
attitude that hinders the growth of others. There are
only two ways to solve this problem. One way is to
reduce the rate of growth, because one person's dis-
proportionate progress disturbs others and offends
them; the other is always to try to find ways to encourage others' growth, so they do not feel that they are
stagnating or regressing in relation to you.

If you find you are advancing too quickly in relation to others and inviting jealousy, you should be
careful to remain modest, especially if you are not particularly skilled in human relations. In other words,
you should not be too proud or boast about your suc-

cesses; instead, continue growing quietly without limits, as if you aim to reach heaven.

In the final stages of success, people usually become reserved and reticent. When they are truly growing, they are less talkative; they become calm and quiet. In many cases, this is when people are about to achieve success. If at this point they become boastful, they will most likely create enemies. As if expecting something to obstruct their success, they talk too much and invite the jealousy of others. There are people who ruin the bud of their own success in this way. However, those who achieve real success are always quiet, move swiftly, and reach their destination without being noticed by others.

Another way to eliminate negativity and lessen the poison of arrogance is to wholeheartedly help others. If you are concerned only with your own growth, it means the vertical factor is too strong and you have forgotten the horizontal factor. At the same time that you aim for your own growth, you should also be willing to encourage infinite development in others. It is important to share the seeds of happiness instead of keeping them to yourself.

5. Sharing, Planting, and Saving Good Fortune
When you become reasonably confident about your own growth and achievements, the next step is to con-

sider gradually spreading the seeds of happiness. If both your hands are full of the seeds of happiness, you should consider sharing them with others. This attitude of sharing happiness or sharing good fortune is important.

What is more, instead of being content with temporary success, you should aim for further development and prosperity extending into the future. To do this, instead of enjoying your present good fortune or happiness to the full, you need to set aside some part of it to invest and plant the seeds for the future.

Another important attitude is saving your good fortune. Even if you have achieved great success, displaying your good fortune and boasting about it will gradually erode your virtue. If you continue in this way, other people will keep their distance. The idea of "saving your good fortune" means valuing and cherishing your success so that it does not slip through your fingers.

An old Chinese story teaches us the dangers of squandering happiness. A young man named Du-zi-chun heard about some buried treasure from an old mountain hermit. The young man found the spot and unearthed an abundance of treasure. Du-zi-chun boasted of his find and word soon spread. Having heard of the young man's good luck, friends and relatives from near and far visited his house. Every day, he gave extravagant banquets and within three years he had exhausted all his treasure.

When people happen to receive wealth beyond their means, they tend to entertain friends excessively and, as a result, will quickly return to their former state. It also happens that if people achieve sudden success, they often find themselves surrounded by flattering new "friends" who wish to take advantage of their good fortune and, before they know it, their fortune is exhausted. These are examples of what happens to those who do not know how to save good fortune.

If you find yourself with an unexpectedly large sum of money, or achieve some unexpected success, be careful not to use all your good fortune straight-away. Limit the amount you spend, and save the rest carefully. It is advisable to use wealth in such a way as to limit your expenditure to an amount you think appropriate for you. Sharing, planting, and saving good fortune are three basic ideas related to wealth also introduced by the Japanese novelist, Rohan Koda (1867–1947).

6. Sharing Your Good Fortune to Nurture Others

There is one more advanced idea to add to the idea of sharing good fortune. It is not enough just to share.

Sharing should also include an element of investment for the future, enabling others to plant the seeds of success for themselves. Not only should you share a part of your money or success with others but you should also consider opening up a path for them so that they can carve their way to prosperity through their own efforts.

If a man becomes rich or successful, his wealth and success can benefit others and shine light on those around him. However, a light that is not a person's own will gradually fade and one day these people will find themselves in the shadows again. If you do not radiate light from within, but only bask in the reflected light of someone else's glory, the time will come when you lose this light. In life, this always happens.

To avoid this, not only should you share good fortune; you should also plant good fortune, that is to say, teach others the spirit of self-help so that in the future when they have to stand on their own, they can radiate light. If you do not do this, sharing your fortune could have a detrimental effect on the future of others. Once people taste easy success, they tend to begin taking advantage of others' hard work, like mosquitoes sucking the blood of other animals, and this can ruin many a promising future.

When you share your fortune with others, watch your own attitude. Do not share your fortune in an attempt to lessen your own feelings of guilt because you alone have been successful. The outcome of sharing good fortune can be either beneficial or harmful depending on your attitude. In an office, for example, you should acknowledge the abilities of others and prepare a path for each appropriate to their growth. You should not think that just because you have been promoted, others should be rewarded equally, nor should you treat everyone equally in order to avoid jealousy in the office. If you always deal with your colleagues in this way, you will gradually lead them to their downfall.

On such occasions, you should put your own emotions aside and take a logical and thoughtful approach so as to nurture others in the long term. What is important is not to give love merely out of sympathy, out of the wish to avoid conflict, or out of pity. Rather, you should show others how they can find their true selves, and develop their full potential.

Evil does not really exist in and of itself; it arises out of a friction between people, place, and time. So if you are about to achieve or have just achieved success, do not fall into raptures. Be wise in sharing your success and wealth, and make an effort to find a way to truly nurture other people.

Chapter Three

A Self-Tormenting Mentality

1. The Beginning of Self-Torment

In this chapter, I would like to discuss the self-tormenting mentality, one of the obstacles to achieving human happiness. A self-tormenting mentality means, as the name suggests, an attitude of persecuting oneself. This is closely connected to pride, which I discussed in the previous chapter, and the inferiority complex that often lies behind pride.

A self-tormenting mentality begins early in life, much earlier than you would expect. In nursery schools, for example, you can already see that certain children are being bullied. The reason for this is that the innate tendencies of the soul become evident very early on in our lives. According to my observations, those children who are frequent victims of bullying seem to have a part of their soul that invites harass-ment. In other words, it seems a tendency that invites bullying has already been formed in past incarnations. A self-tormenting mentality arises from both this sort of innate tendency and also as a result of experiences in this life.

2. Self-Torment as an Innate Tendency

Let us first look at the innate factors that determine our mental attitudes. Why are certain children treated badly by their peers, and why are others bullies? Although it is not possible to say that children are evil by nature, it does seem some children have an urge to bully others. When I look for the reason for this, I find that children who are on the receiving end of bullying are very vulnerable or, rather, it seems almost as though they expect to be hurt. This negative tendency can be described as a shadow of unhappiness that hangs over them. They tend to be over-anxious and always think in a negative way.

If you analyze the type of children who are vulner-able, you will find they have obvious weaknesses that are likely to make them targets of attack. Perhaps, for example, their speech is awkward or their actions slow. They may be badly dressed or always have runny noses; they may have rashes, warts, or pimples.

Physical weaknesses are often the reason these children become targets of abuse; however, this kind of abuse does not continue forever. On the other hand, there are others who are constantly teased and bullied, as if there was something within them inviting attack. The reason for this is that their thoughts are directed inward; in other words they are introverted as opposed to outgoing.

People rarely criticize those who have a lot of confidence and strength of will. These sorts of people give the impression that if criticized, they would return an attack without hesitation. If you punched someone like this, he or she would throw five or six punches in return. In this way, you do not dare criticize this sort of person for fear the criticism will rebound on you. Although human thoughts are invisible, you are actually daunted by the strength of the person's will.

Those who are self-tormenting, in contrast, give the impression that they might burst into tears at the first blow, and are expecting another two or three punches. They show too easily that they are weak and so invite further attack. This tendency could be described as a kind of masochism, but the root is actually deeper than that. They may be souls who have been hurt many times in past lives; they may have received little love or been tortured a great deal; they may also have tormented themselves.

In discussing the self-tormenting mentality, I would like to point out that some people do have an innate tendency to torment themselves. Everyone can check for this trait by reflecting on their own childhood. Check and see if you had this kind of negative tendency when you were a child. Even if you did, it is possible to overcome it. However, some people as adults still have the same tendencies they had in childhood and they continue to be easy targets for bullies. I strongly advise you to use this thought to analyze your character. If you are constantly bullied, you should not blame the bully but understand that you, too, are responsible, as you probably have a mental tendency that invites attacks.

3. Self-Torment as a Tendency Acquired in This Lifetime

Now I would like to discuss the reason that certain people are likely to be bullied and develop a self-tormenting mentality as a result of experiences in this life. Why are people hard on themselves? There seem to be two main reasons this sort of tendency develops.

The first is repeated failure. When failure and disappointment are experienced again and again, it is human nature to anticipate further failure. People tend to think that, by anticipating the extent of the pain they are likely to experience before something actually happens, they are better prepared to deal with it. It is the same as doing a forward roll on a mat; beforehand we tell all our muscles to get ready for the roll. Or, before vaulting over a box, we tell our bodies to get ready to jump. Similarly, even before we actually experience failure, we often tell ourselves to brace for a shock in order to lessen the impact. We know only too well that if we fall from a height it will be painful, so we need to learn the knack of breaking a fall or, as in judo, learn how to fall without hurting ourselves. This psychological breaking of falls tends to turn into a self-tormenting mentality. If people experience failure many times, they are likely to form the habit of preparing themselves for shocks they anticipate.

However, some people who have open, cheerful characters do not mind if they experience failure. These types of people are not too attached to past failure. In contrast, the sort of people who cannot easily forget past failure could be described as delicate and vulnerable. Because they are so sensitive, they are easily hurt and, to a large extent, this sensitivity is part of their innate character. It is true that such delicate souls often become artists or writers, because only sensitive souls can appreciate subtlety. Unfortunately, however, if this sensitivity works in a negative way, the sensitive person becomes apprehensive and constantly comes to expect failure rather than success. In this way a gloomy, somber personality develops.

If you have this sort of vulnerability, first you need to accept this fact objectively. You have formed a tendency to torment yourself because, after numerous experiences of failure, you are afraid of failing yet again, and out of this fear you prepare yourself for imminent failure. Understanding this is the first step to overcoming this mentality. Next, you need to assess the probability that you will fail again. Logically, your chances of success and your chances of failure are equal. The probability of failure cannot be more than fifty percent. However, if you envision failure and come to expect it, strangely enough you will find yourself making choices that lead to failure. Unfortunately, this mindset results in attracting failure to yourself and causing it to happen.

Now let us discuss the second reason a self-tormenting mentality develops. As well as those who have experienced many failures in the past, people who are essentially competent and outstanding may also develop this sort of mentality. In a spiritual sense, they are giants, and their power is so great that nothing can contain their inner strength. However, in order to lead a normal life on Earth, they have had to suppress their great strength and with difficulty they have done this. As a result, to ease the pain of living an earthly life, a self-tormenting mentality tends to develop.

The nobler the soul and the greater its caliber, the less easily it adapts to life on Earth. Because great souls know their own true stature in the depths of their heart, they cannot help feeling that they are being treated unreasonably in this world. If they have high social status, highly developed abilities, and enough power to accomplish great tasks in this world, they may be able to stand up and fight to abolish some of the absurdities in society. They can use their power to fight social ills and build a better world.

However, to be able to accomplish this kind of task in this world they need to accumulate sufficient strength, otherwise everything they think and do may work against them. This is because there is too big a gap between where they ought to be, in the light of their essential greatness of soul or spiritual level, and the reality they must accept in society. As they see everything going against their hopes and aspirations and feel they are being treated badly, great souls may start to worry that they are actually far inferior to everyone else, or that they are incapable of adapting to reality. In times of trouble, great souls are likely to develop a self-tormenting mentality. Often this is temporary, but sometimes these sorts of negative tendencies persist and increase and then such souls begin to doubt their abilities and talents. If they feel incapable of adapting to reality, they may conclude that reality is right and they are wrong.

The reason many great souls develop a self-tormenting mentality is often that they have had painful experiences in their youth. Because they have such high aspirations and ideals, such exalted desires and hopes, they cannot accommodate themselves to the reality of life on Earth, and as a result they experience feelings of helplessness and disappointment. Through objective eyes, however, what they regard as failure is not as serious as they imagine. Because their ideals are so high and their aspirations so strong, they are suffocated by circumstances which to most people appear quite ordinary, and they feel as if they are enduring a grave failure.

To sum up, there are two types of people who have a self-tormenting mentality. The first are those who have developed this mentality through many experiences of failure, and the second type are essentially great souls who have difficulty adapting to the earthly world.

4. Remedies for a Self-Tormenting Mentality (1)

Let us now think about how to overcome a self-tormenting mentality. There is a question I would like to ask people of the first type, those who have developed a self-tormenting mentality as the result of repeated experiences of failure and the ensuing disappointment, or through an overwhelming challenge that has left them suffering an inferiority complex. Do you really believe you are entitled to happiness? These people actually seem to believe they do not deserve happiness.

As I have explained in Chapter One, human beings have the ability to choose happiness or unhappiness. This ability is dependent on understanding that *you* must make a decision about whether you wish to be happy or unhappy. If you have experienced failures that have resulted in disappointment, if you have developed a tendency to focus on the negative aspects of a situation and have come to feel that no matter what you try to do you will fail, ask yourself whether this way of thinking will bring you happiness in the future. If you expect failure and talk openly about it until finally it becomes a reality, will that bring you happiness? Is that what you really want? I would like you to ask yourself these questions sincerely and understand that happiness will never come to you unless you can find a satisfactory answer to these questions.

If you find any signs of self-torment in yourself, know that it is like dirt, like gravel or sand that has gotten into your clothes. Remove this irritation as quickly as possible. The gold dust found in silt shines, but if the flakes of gold are covered by large quantities of sand, their true value will not be recognized. To find the gold, you must sift the silt through a sieve. If you do not make this effort, you will not be able to recognize what is truly of value. Similarly, you have to get rid of the "silt" within yourself, the tendency to focus on the negative aspects, a self-tormenting mentality that infiltrates the kingdom within. These sorts of impurities are like a cancer eating into the future and destroying it. You must not create negative thoughts or allow them to pass your lips.

If dark thoughts come into your mind, make a clear distinction between what has happened in the past, what is happening in the present, and what will happen in the future. Even if you have experienced failure before, there is no reason for you to fail this time or repeat any similar failure in the future.

Imagine a man who always carries an umbrella and says there is no telling when it might rain. What do you think of his attitude? If you saw him carrying a large umbrella on a fine, sunny morning, wouldn't you think that absurd? Ask him why he carries an umbrella, he will frown and answer, "Although it is perfectly sunny now, sooner or later the sky will cloud over and it is bound to rain, so if I carry an umbrella every day I will always be prepared for rain. That's why." Nevertheless, you sense he is somehow annoyed by the fact that he has to carry a heavy umbrella day after day. Wouldn't you think his behavior ridiculous?

People who have a self-tormenting mentality are exactly like this man with the umbrella. No matter how sunny it is, no matter what the weather forecast says, they insist that it will rain eventually, so they never leave their umbrellas behind. No matter how much others ridicule them, these people stick to their own opinions. They focus on all the rainy days in the past, and if they happen to encounter unexpected rain, as probably happens a few times a year, they feel satisfied because their prediction was correct. Even if you point out to them that the other three hundred and sixty days have been sunny, any attempt to convince them will be useless. They will feel satisfied that they are right because it has rained five times in the past year! If you think that this example applies to other people and not to you, you will simply laugh it off; however, in actual fact, it applies to every single person.

If you see a similar tendency in yourself, why not change it? Although it may well be raining today, that does not mean it will rain tomorrow as well. Tomorrow may be perfect weather and, besides, is there anything wrong with expecting a fine day? It does not make sense to worry about carrying an umbrella if tomorrow might be sunny. You should let go of this mental burden as soon as possible.

5. Remedies for a Self-Tormenting Mentality (2)

Next, I would like to discuss the second type of people who have a self-tormenting mentality—those who are essentially great souls. The ultimate expression of self-torment and self-punishment must be to die a martyr. It seems that many great souls have had a hidden wish to die on the cross. However, this tendency is unhealthy.

Sometimes human beings encounter severe trials that are intended by heaven to enrich and refine their souls. Through the process of enduring such trials, a soul is actually strengthened, like steel that is tempered by heating and sudden cooling. However, focusing too much on the value of trials and difficulties may lead to the glorifying of ordeals. As a result, you may come to feel that you must bear the entire weight of human sin upon your own shoulders. There are some

truly great souls who have an acut(
feel the weight of all the sins of hu\
feel responsible for all of humanity's \
all evil since the beginning of time; the
their mission to shoulder the heavy burd
responsibility with tears in their eyes and .
their foreheads, reducing themselves to the likes (
pack-horses or mules.

There is, perhaps, a certain justification for expecting to have to undergo severe ordeals. Indeed, great
souls often do experience severe testing. However,
even if difficult situations arise, the response of great
souls varies, depending on the attitudes of the individual. Although in essence they may be angels of light,
each will respond to an ordeal in a different way. If
you constantly expect that trials and tribulations will
befall you, when a difficulty actually occurs it will
seem much more serious than it really is because you
have a belief that the severer the hardship, the more
God expects of you. Unfortunately, people with these
expectations are not likely to be successful in this
world.

The difference between great souls who succeed
and those who do not lies in the value that they attach
to hardship. For those who believe hardship to be
essential in their lives, difficulties will materialize to

overwhelm them. On the other hand, for those who see difficulties as insubstantial and believe that hardship is given to strengthen their soul and enhance its gifts, to serve as a springboard for the next step in life, trials will seem like big waves that can be surfed. The question is whether you see life's difficulties as substantial and overwhelming or as waves that you can ride with ease; in other words, whether you can surf the waves or whether you are pulled under by the current. Even if you are essentially a great soul, I recommend that you do not glorify hardship but rather glean from it pearls of wisdom that contribute to your spiritual wealth.

There have been a number of angels of light who have died tragic deaths, and I believe the reason for this was a self-tormenting mentality that attracted negativity. Many angels have been assassinated. This was perhaps inevitable in some cases; if a person has an extremely strong wish to save the world, even at the expense of his or her own life, that person often invites hardship.

Great souls who have difficulty adapting to the reality of this life on Earth have two different ways of coping with the conflict between the reality of the material world and the reality of the soul. The first way is to yield to reality; the second is to endeavor to bring reality closer to their high ideals. If they attempt to compromise with reality at the expense of their ideals, tragedy inevitably follows. If, on the other hand, they endeavor to bring reality closer to their ideals, they will find that reality can be molded in the direction of their ideals.

If you think you are one of those great souls who have a self-tormenting mentality, listen carefully to my advice. It will take a great deal of time and effort to turn ideals into reality. You must go through many processes, so do not adopt an uncompromising, all-or-nothing stance; instead, always think of practical ways to realize your dreams. Then, take steady steps, one at a time, toward your goals. As you keep advancing in this way, the stormy waves of life's difficulties will quiet and the sea will once again become calm. Instead of tormenting yourself, endeavor to achieve success in this earthly world.

A sense of guilt about worldly success often gives rise to self-torment. If you think that worldly success is against the will of God or that you should not live peacefully and happily as long as there is even one person in the world who is in pain or poverty, this way of thinking will inevitably invite self-punishment. It is important to forgive yourself with generosity and a peaceful mind. Great souls are able to forgive other people and this is often their most important mission. However, they tend not to be very good at forgiving themselves. This reveals a narrow-mindedness arising out of their stoical attitude to life. So, try to forgive not only others but also yourself.

Forgiving yourself means believing that you are one of God's children, that you are a manifestation of His power. A child of God should not be miserable. This holds especially true for those who have the potential to be leaders. If a leader gradually becomes more and more unhappy, what will happen to those who follow? Understand and engrave deeply in your mind that it is not only your right but your duty to attain happiness in this life.

A self-tormenting mentality is a mental tendency that invites unhappiness. No matter how hard you try, no one, not even God, can save the person who chooses to be unhappy. So, if you have this tendency, look up at the sun in the sky. Even if it is raining now, believe that the sun will come out again. It is my wish for everyone to create a wonderful life.

PART TWO

Chapter One

One Chance in a Million

1. The First Step to a New Life

The Institute for Research in Human Happiness is at a new stage in its development, overflowing with hope. Books of the Truth are being distributed worldwide, and the name of our Institute is becoming increasingly well-known throughout the world.

Now, there is a ray of powerful light before our eyes, and I am determined to follow this wholeheartedly. How should we follow this path of light? Although each person may have unresolved personal problems, now that the guiding hand has been raised (as the basic sutra of our Institute *The Dharma of the Right Mind* describes) it is important for each individual to be determined to follow this hand and continue without stopping on this path of light.

New Year is the time when we have the chance to rediscover the significance of the annual cycle. If God has granted us the yearly cycle in which to lead our human lives, it is our duty to value this cycle and make the best of it. This means that every year we must resolve to make a fresh start on a new life. The reason God created one year cycles is that through these cycles, He expected us to have more opportunities for spiritual growth. God could have created a yearlong spring, summer, autumn, and winter; we could have had four-year cycles. However, this would have slowed our lives considerably, thus slowing the evolution of the human soul. I believe that the twelve months in a year is the optimal period for spiritual refinement.

At the beginning of the year, you should not miss the opportunity to reflect on your life over the past twelve months. In the past year, how much have you transformed yourself after studying the Truth? How did you spend your time, and are you proud of the way you lived your life? Did you study and understand the Truth fully? Did you have any wrong thoughts? Did you act against the teachings knowingly? Please reflect on these things carefully.

As a new year is about to begin, this is the time for high hopes and the time to start marching forward. Based on what you discover through reflecting on the previous year, draw up a plan for the new one. Those who study the Truth must keep in mind at the very least the following two points.

First, you need to achieve personal happiness. By this I do not mean living in an egotistical way; in fact, what I am talking about is far from a selfish way of life. "Happiness" is another name for enlightenment, which helps individuals to build a strong inner self, to develop greater stature, to become capable of receiving the Light of God, and to spread this Light to the world. In short, personal happiness is the sense of happiness that you feel when you receive God's Light, understand His mission, and fulfill sacred tasks according to His will.

You are a child of God who originated in Him. This is the essence of being human. When you savor the joy of being a child of God, you attain personal happiness, and there is no limit to how much of this happiness you can experience. As long as it is happiness at being a child of God, no matter how happy you become, it will not harm others.

Personal happiness, then, becomes the power to bring happiness to others and to society, and to promote the creation of an ideal world. Your happiness becomes the happiness of the majority, and this creates a great whirlpool of happiness in society. This is the second point, achieving collective happiness. To sum up, the very first step in starting a new life in the New Year is to uphold the pursuit of infinite happiness, both personal and collective.

2. Check on Your Daily Life

I would like to look again at the importance of a single day. At the beginning of the year in particular, we sense the value of a day, and this is the most appropriate time to think about how to live to the fullest within the framework of one day. There is no other time of year when we see each day with such fresh eyes and feel grateful for the twenty-four hours that God has given us.

Do not think of your time as something that belongs solely to you. Your day is precious time that God has entrusted to you. Some people may believe that they are free to decide how to use the twenty-four hours in a day, but in most cases their time is spent ruled by laziness. This is because their interpretation of time is mistaken. The truth is that every day, twenty-four hours are given to everyone, and the question is constantly being asked: What have you done in these twenty-four hours? So, first, it is important to change your perspective of time. The time you have is not yours, it has been entrusted or given to you. Once you truly understand this, you will know what you need to do.

Banks are entrusted with the money of many customers and people take it for granted that once they deposit their money in a bank they will receive interest. However, if banks merely left the money sitting in safes, they could not pay their customers any interest. It is the duty of banks to invest the money they are entrusted with to create greater value and increase their profits so that they can give customers some return on their money.

This is just one example, but something similar can be said of each of us. God gives us twenty-four hours a day and using these hours we are supposed to create something that is of much greater value than just these twenty-four hours. Otherwise, just like a bank that merely puts the deposits in a safe, if we continue paying interest we will go bankrupt. The fact that we have twenty-four hours a day indicates that God deposits the same amount of money called "time" with each of us, and once we have been entrusted with it we have to pay Him back some interest.

The "interest" we have to pay means the work we do that is of service to the world, even to a small extent. What does it mean, then, to serve the world? It is giving love to others and practicing altruism. The reason we have to give love is that the actions of love are regarded as the interest we owe God. Because we are given twenty-four hours a day, each day we have to pay back a certain amount of interest to God, otherwise the money called "time" that God has deposited will be wasted.

If we continue wasting His deposit, we cannot complain if God decides to take our time away, saying, "The twenty-four hours that I invested in you were completely lost, so I will no longer deposit time with you, I will give it to someone else." To prevent this from happening, we need to value the time that we are given, and be willing to pay back the interest called love.

To pay back interest, you should not just spend time doing whatever you like; instead, you need to invest your time in something more valuable and, by doing so, produce something wonderful. Your achievements will then be given back to you as personal happiness, and you will feel great joy. At the same time, what you have achieved will bring joy to others, and they will share in a collective happiness.

As a result, both your personal happiness and the collective happiness of others will become a source of joy for God; in this way, by spreading happiness, you can pay Him back the interest.

3. Three-Step Thinking

For those who are thinking of making a plan for the New Year, I would like to introduce a new way of thinking that I have named "three-step thinking." Generally speaking, the human mind is familiar with categories of thinking, either the dichotomy of yes and no, or the three levels—high, middle and low. In creating a New-Year's plan, I would like to recommend that you use three-step thinking.

Let me explain what three-step thinking is. The first step is to think about the negative aspects of your life. When you look back at the way you have lived so far, you will find a negative part of yourself that consists of what goes against the Truth, what prevents you from achieving happiness as a child of God, and what obstructs the happiness of others. First, it is important to look squarely at the negative aspects of your character and constantly try to reduce these, turning them into positive attributes.

Those who do not make the effort to check on their mistakes and their defects, who do not correct them and turn them into positive attributes, will not achieve ultimate success. The following example illustrates this. Suppose a man is mopping the floor with a bucket of clear water. As he dips his mop into the bucket again and again, the water becomes dirty. He changes the water and continues mopping, but what if there is a leak in the bottom of the bucket? Although he believes he is cleaning the long corridor with a clean mop, there are pools of dirty water leaking from the bucket. As long as he continues mopping in this way, the corridor will never become clean.

To take another example, there are people who when they clean, are content just to sweep the dust out of sight. Many simply move the dust from the space in front of them to collect in another place. When they invite guests, for instance, they put the things that are not needed in the next room and just clean the room they are going to use. These types of people do not clean their whole house completely, they just cover up what is dirty.

The same goes for the negative parts within you. Unless you get rid of the negativity, you cannot really achieve spiritual growth. It is important not to accumulate negativity within you, or spread it outside. Always check and see what the negative aspects of your character are and try to eliminate them. Before you take action, make sure that thoughts and actions will not result in any negative outcomes.

The next step is to follow the Middle Way, a balanced way. You need to check that what you are going to do accords with the spirit of the Middle Way, that is to say it does not go to extremes and does it not destroy harmony. Not only should you check that you have not created any negativity in a day, but you also need to look at your thoughts and actions from the perspective of the Middle Way. You may make the excuse that you had no choice except to do something in a certain way, but you need to take another look at your behavior from the standpoint of the Middle Way.

The Middle Way is the path that leads to infinite development, and achieves great harmony after eliminating the two extremes. It is the path that enables everyone, be it a teacher, a follower, a superior, or a subordinate, to live their life to the fullest while fulfilling their role. This path not only allows for your own progress. It also helps others, nurturing both parties and opening up infinite possibilities for them. To enter the Middle Way, you need to avoid intense emotional agitation and behaviors that are too extreme. The Middle Way is the path to human perfection, the path to becoming a person of greater stature. So please check your thoughts and deeds in the light of this concept.

Once you find that your thoughts and deeds accord with the spirit of the Middle Way, you should then check the positive and constructive aspects of your character. While entering the Middle Way, where you harm neither yourself nor others, you also need to produce something positive, of benefit to both parties. Check and see whether you can benefit yourself and others by reconciling the interests of both parties, and create new values centered on the Middle Way. I call this "positive thinking with the Middle Way as the foundation." Human thoughts and deeds always generate some outcome, and it is vital to ascertain that this outcome will be positive.

When you decide on your goals for a year, I would like you to follow these three steps. First is the negative approach, which is checking that you are not creating anything that will have a negative effect. Second is the approach of the Middle Way, which is checking that you have gotten rid of extremes. Third is the positive approach, checking to see that you create something positive that benefits not only yourself but others as well, and above all else, God.

You can produce positive outcomes by practicing the Middle Way. If you enthusiastically attempt to create something positive without a balanced foundation, it is highly possible that you will harm either yourself or others—so please value these steps. I would like you always to use this three-step thinking, focusing particularly on the Middle Way, and achieve progress on this path.

4. How to Invite Miracles

After you have drawn up a plan for the New Year based on this three-step thinking, as the next step it is important to change your view of yourself. Once you decide to study the Truth, you will no longer be the same person you used to be. You become someone special, who has been awakened in order to realize God's ideals on Earth. Although you still inhabit a human body and are subject to physical conditions, you are no longer a "normal" person; you become someone armed with sacred treasures handed down from God so that you can open up a path before you. Everything you have, including your sword, your bow and arrow, your shield, and your pike have been entrusted to you by God. When you realize this, a completely new world will unfold before your very eyes.

Joining our Institute means signing a kind of contract with God—in other words, making a promise to God that you will live to realize His ideals on Earth and be part of this movement. When you enter into this agreement, you will experience many miracles that would not be possible if your perspective was solely materialistic. Although "faith" may be a well-worn word, its true value is the strong determination to fulfill the promise you have made to God, no matter what the cost.

The actions of faith accompany a belief in God, so you should not be content just to express your belief in Him in words. Your beliefs need to be expressed in actions, and this is the meaning of "believing is acting." I assure you that when you express your faith in actions, miracles will happen. God will open up a path for those who respect the contract they have made and who are trying to fulfill it. Those who join our Institute sign a contract with God, with the grand aim of manifesting His ideals.

You will experience many miracles. Because God is everything and He is almighty, everything becomes possible. Faith is what makes the impossible possible. It is the determination to carry out your mission resolutely and with courage; as long as you hold to this resolution, every obstacle will be cleared away. If you make a promise to God and you decide to take action to keep your promise, I declare that you will experience many miracles.

5. One Chance in a Million

To end this chapter, I would like to give you a gift in the form of the phrase, "one chance in a million." What does this phrase mean? Here, one million signifies a long period of time, a million years, so this phrase suggests an opportunity that might come within your reach only once in a million years.

You are now being given a chance that you may not encounter for another million years—the chance to increase your level of enlightenment. Whether or not you can take hold of this opportunity for yourself and generate positive results totally depends on the effort you make. I give many kinds of teachings on the Truth, but unless you make sure you have mastered them for yourself these teachings will not become a part of you.

When you read books of the Truth, remember the phrase, "one chance in a million." When you have the chance to attend a lecture or a meditation seminar at our Institute, recall the phrase, "one chance in a million." Once you truly understand the meaning of this phrase, you cannot but become a completely different person. You will experience an enlightenment that has the power to change a person. It is my strong hope that you become aware of the scales covering your eyes and remove them, taking a great leap forward and making progress year after year.

Chapter Two

An Indomitable Spirit

1. Summon Your Willpower

In this chapter, I would like to talk about indomitable spirit. In the depths of winter, it seems as though Mother Nature is trying to strengthen our frail wills. This is the time when we most need to summon our willpower and think about what we need to do.

Summoning energy is easier said than done. You may be able to talk about it but, in reality, it is hard to keep your energy levels up constantly. Knowing this, however, I must tell you that to be successful in life you need to exert willpower when necessary; otherwise success will never be yours. Willpower is a key factor in achieving success in life.

Look at those who are successful in the world. All of them are filled with energy. Where in the world do you find successful people with downcast, bleary eyes and sagging shoulders? There are certain characteristics that energetic people share. They are all strongly determined to endure hardship and overcome difficulties. Those who can find and use the energy within when difficulties or hardships arise will be able to overcome them to succeed; however, those who become weak or cowardly in the face of difficulties will never be successful.

When people lead uneventful lives without any serious problems, they tend to feel weakened and trapped in lives of repetition and mediocrity. However, when something unexpected happens, an earth-shaking event that awakens them from sleep, they feel all their muscles and nerves suddenly revitalized. Indeed, it is not in times of mediocrity but in the face of adversity, when confronted by difficulties and hardships, that the soul is able to rise to the challenge, radiating a brilliant light.

So in the deepest winter in your life, in the harshest, coldest season of your soul, what will you do? The first thing you need to know and understand is that a life lived without strong willpower is a life of defeat. The life you are living at present gains significance only if you activate your strength of will. It is no exaggeration to say that if you do not use the energy of willpower, your life will be of no real significance and no true value. What I would like to say is this: Above all else, summon the willpower to act.

2. Use Your Intellectual Powers to the Utmost
Secondly, I would like to emphasize the importance of using your intellectual powers. It is, of course, very important to summon willpower, but if you forget to use your wisdom you may well be wasting your energy. For instance, even if you are eager to undergo an esoteric Buddhist training, if you choose the wrong goals your energy will be wasted. I have to say that your efforts will be in vain if you are satisfied with climbing mountains, standing under waterfalls, or fasting for the sole purpose of trying to draw attention to yourself.

Life lasts for not many decades, eighty or ninety years at the most. During this short span, how can you make the best possible use of your time? It is extremely important to view your life from a perspective of how to use it to the fullest. You must waste no time; so first, try to use your intellectual powers. It is important to rack your brains and think about how to make the best of your life, making each day the best you possibly can until your life shines.

Intellectual power is the ability to produce new ideas constantly. I often talk about the importance of trying to improve oneself, of generating new ideas and looking out for discoveries and new inventions day after day. Each and every person makes different discoveries and thinks of different inventions, and the value of a lifetime depends on the quality of these discoveries and inventions. It may be valuable to work up a sweat; however, unless you work in a way that truly helps others, your life could end up empty.

While leading an energetic life, you need to refine and direct your energy by using wisdom. It is very important to use your intelligence for what truly has value and what truly brings happiness to others and not to waste your energy on what is not important. As I said before, intellectual power is the continual effort to discover and invent, day after day. You will surely make your own discoveries and inventions. It cannot be true that in a lifetime you will come up with no new ideas. If you look back and feel unfulfilled, or sense that something important is missing, this means that your inner self is telling you to use your intellect. If you use your intellectual powers fully, you should be able to do meaningful work and lead a more meaningful life. Do not ever forget to use your intellectual powers.

3. Stand up Resolutely

I have talked about the importance of willpower and intelligence. What I would like to speak about next is taking a step forward. Once you have become enthusiastic and developed good ideas, confront any problems, then proceed to the next stage. It is important to actually create something new.

Everyone must have at least one moment in their life when they decide to take a brave stand. If you look back at your life and you cannot find any such moment, you have had a sad life. When you stand up resolutely, light bursts forth from within. This is also the moment when courage bursts through, resolving any difficult problems.

Many people find themselves trapped in the midst of worries. Nevertheless, viewed from a spiritual perspective, they are like Gulliver caught in Lilliput, the land of little people. Lying on his back, Gulliver was fastened with strings and pegs to the ground but, had he really wanted to, he could easily have broken the strings, wrenched out the pegs, and stood up to free himself. If Gulliver had taken a brave stand, the Lilliputians would have scattered and fled.

You have probably lost sight of yourself as a giant, and delude yourself that you have been caught by tiny Lilliputians; however, you should not let that situation continue. Raise your right arm, your left arm, your legs, and push yourself up off the ground. Loosen the strings that bind you and resolutely stand up. This is the key to solving major problems in life. As long as you try to escape from them without doing anything, you will not be able to find a way through. I would especially like to emphasize that being dependent on others and constantly seeking help is risky.

Why not summon the strength to stand on your own two feet and try to solve your problems yourself? Why not try to advance into the ice like an icebreaker? If an icebreaker stops moving forward, it soon becomes stuck, frozen in ice. You should not be like that. You must be brave and move forward, for who else is going to save you from the problems of this world?

When you stand up bravely and take action, a halo encircles you and the angels in the heavenly world are filled with delight. Cast off the mindset of constantly looking back with regret, bound by past events, and, instead, take a new step forward. As I get to know more people, I find that many are content to lead easy lives. So many people are attached to past glory, success, their reputation, or their status that they refuse to get out of tepid water, squatting down in it despite the fact that the vast world of Truth is exposed before their very eyes. Do not remain like that. Rather, stake your life on the Truth and live with passion. Stand up and fight for the Truth. What else could be more important? I want to emphasize the importance of standing up resolutely, and devoting your life to the Truth.

4. Do Not Give in to Negative Spiritual Influences
The next important topic that I would like to explore is spiritual influences. There are many different prescriptions for solving problems in life, but one factor that should never be ignored is negative spiritual influences.

Whether or not we are aware of it, it is a fact that we are affected by spiritual influences in our daily lives. Most people come under negative spiritual influences and are affected by invisible temptations. The cause of this is what are known as "stray spirits," spirits who once lived as human beings, worried and suffered the same sorts of problems that most people have, but who left this world before they were able to solve them. Their negative thoughts or vibrations are transmitted to you because the same negativity exists within yourself and is attracting them.

The existence of stray spirits gives rise to many questions. Every time I see or feel them, I wonder why human beings, dignified as they are, have to suffer in this way. I question why these spirits continue such foolish and shameful behavior, taking possession of people on Earth and making them suffer even more. But these spirits have their own way of thinking, and they do not know how to get out of their present state. These spirits are not aware of the truth of the existence of the spirit world. The only thing on their minds is this earthly world, a world they are still trying to live in. They want to live in this material world for all eternity, so despite the fact that they no longer have physical bodies, without realizing or without even wanting to be aware that they have already died, they try to satisfy their desires by possessing people on Earth.

When you are aware that you have come under these sorts of negative spiritual influences, you need to let these spirits know what a mistake they are making and how wrong their behavior is. It is necessary to teach them that as long as they try to possess or influence people on Earth in a negative way, they can never be happy, because by doing so, they are only creating more wrongdoing. As their mistakes accumulate, they suffer even more, and by making living people suffer as well, their suffering increases endlessly.

Keeping this in mind, do not give in to these spirits. Instead, have the courage to make them realize their mistake. It is also an act of love to teach them how wrong it is to possess and delude people living on Earth. You need to search for and find the right way to live as a human being. To provide these spirits with the opportunity to reflect on their thoughts and deeds instead of being controlled by them, it is essential that you yourself emit a brilliant light.

To prevent stray spirits from coming into existence and to create a world where no such spirits are able to exert any influence, it is necessary that everyone be determined to observe the following three points. First, have a firm faith in the existence of God. A truly wonderful world begins with believing. Have faith in God and also believe in guiding spirits in the heavenly world. When the Laws of Truth are taught, it is important to be connected to the Truth by taking refuge in the Dharma. These attitudes are the very thoughts that tie you to God with a golden rope, protecting you from all sorts of negative spiritual influences.

Those who have lost the will to take refuge in the Dharma will lose hold of the rope and will have to overcome negative influences on their own. When fighting to be rid of negative spiritual influences, it is important to take refuge in the Dharma and tie your-self firmly to the golden rope from God.

Secondly, you should devote yourself fully to the practice of love that gives. When you give love, you should not forget about purity of soul. You must express love in your thoughts and actions with pure motives. If you give love with motives that are not pure, that love will not benefit anyone; it will do you no good nor the person receiving it. It is important to offer love selflessly, with pure intentions.

The third thing you need when fighting to over-come negative spiritual influences is gratitude for the fact that God has given you life. Among those stray spirits I have come into contact with, it was very clear that not a single one had a sense of gratitude. To be born human and lead a life without gratitude is so sad. Living with a grateful heart indicates that you are dis-covering many blessings in life; it shows that you have enough room in your mind to appreciate what is around you. When you have gratitude, you radiate light from within.

When fighting against negative spiritual influ-ences, I would like you to remember the following truth. Stray spirits have disturbed hearts, they are full of complaints, grievances, and unfulfilled desires. Looking back, everyone without exception will find they have experienced these sorts of feelings in the course of their lives. However, as long as you remember to fill your heart with gratitude, something stray spirits never do, you will be able to find your way out to a different wavelength. If your mind is constantly agitated and overwhelmed by feelings of misfortune, it is highly likely that you have come under negative spiritual influences, so please remember this word, "gratitude." When you have a grateful heart, you will no longer be the victim of negative spiritual influences.

5. An Indomitable Spirit

Lastly, I would like to talk about having an indomitable spirit. It is not so difficult to keep seeking the Laws of Truth and studying them. Along the way, however, there are various traps and temptations that await human beings.

Everyone experiences temptations unique to their own soul, for example, a desire for fame, or a desire to be respected by others. A desire for the opposite sex, deep-rooted emotions such as jealousy, and financial problems can also constitute temptations. Everyone without exception, even those who are seeking the Truth and undergoing spiritual discipline, face at least one or two types of temptation.

At the Institute for Research in Human Happiness, members are encouraged to reach the state of Arhat,[1] a level of awareness equivalent to that of the inhabitants of the upper realm of the sixth dimension in the spirit world. However, to progress from the state of Arhat to that of Bodhisattva[2] of the seventh dimension, everyone without exception must overcome one or two temptations. These experiences are great ordeals, but without getting through these ordeals, it is impossible to reach the state of Bodhisattva.

There are times when your soul is tested and polished. The kinds of temptations you face differ from one person to the next, but everyone faces major obstacles or attachments in the course of seeking the Truth and undergoing spiritual refinement. At these times, it is important to be aware that you are being tempted.

How can you overcome these temptations? Always go back to the starting point. It is important to be will-

---

1. Arhat is a word originated from Sanskrit that describes angels who are studying to attain the state of Bodhisattva, working to clear the stains from their minds. Having corrected their mistakes through self-examination, halos form behind their heads. The Japanese word for Arhat is Arakan. Refer to *The Laws of Eternity* by Ryuho Okawa (Lantern Books, 2001), pp. 64–66.

2. Bodhisattva is a word originated from Sanskrit that describes angels who reside in the seventh dimension of the Real World. A Bodhisattva dedicates him- or herself to enlightening and saving people through the will of Buddha. The Japanese word for Bodhisattva is Bosatsu. Refer to *The Laws of Eternity*, Chapter 4: The World of the Seventh Dimension.

ing to let go of everything you have so far accumulated, to want to start afresh with a clean slate at any time, and to remember your original resolution. Even those who have been seeking the Truth and undergone a lot of spiritual discipline sometimes become bound or attached to their own practice. Some become attached to their status while others get attached to the amount of discipline they have undergone. There are also those who are attached to the strength of their faith. There are all sorts of attachments, but everyone inevitably faces some sort of temptation.

At such times, ask yourself if you are able to let go of what you believe you have attained or understood and with a clean slate start your life afresh, without any attachments. Since you started your life from zero, you can start over again from zero at any time. If you can think in this way, the future will eventually open up before you. It might not happen right away, but a path will gradually open up. You may have chosen a difficult path, but it will surely lead you to the golden path.

I hope that many people will come through to have an indomitable spirit, after struggling and overcoming different kinds of hardships. Look at salmon, how they leap waterfalls, swim against rapids, and continue to make their way upstream. Following their example, try to leap the waterfalls, swim against the rapids, and travel upstream to reach a state where your spirit becomes indomitable. I hope more and more people will be able to attain this state. I pray from the depths of my heart that, every year, a great number of people will develop an indomitable spirit.

Chapter Three

An Incomparably Pure Spirit

1. The Home of Souls
In early spring, flowers of different colors burst into bloom all around us. Every year, without fail, spring comes, and I fancy I am not the only one to feel excited at its approach. I am sure many people like spring and feel grateful for the fact that they can experience it over and over again in the course of their lives.

It is in spring that I often remember the faraway home of my soul. A long time ago in early spring, when I was in my spiritual home, I had been contemplating one specific theme. You may wonder where the home of souls is. It is actually the spirit world you inhabited before you were born into this world. In that world too, I was engaged in many different kinds of work and constantly contemplating how happiness could manifest in concrete ways. The original form of happiness is a concept that exists in the highest realm of the spirit world, the Real World, and as it comes down to the lower realms, it manifests in a number of forms. When I was still in the spirit world, I constantly contemplated the concept of happiness and gave serious thought to the matter of how to realize happiness on Earth when I descended.

There is one attitude often observed in the home of souls but not seen on Earth. What do you think that might be? It is something that people do not think seriously about in this earthly world, although in the spirit world thinking about it is a matter of course. This is the habit of thinking about happiness. This habit leads naturally to ideas about how to nurture others, how to bring others happiness, and how to guide others so that they can lead lives filled with joy. In the heavenly world, thinking about happiness is synonymous with bringing others happiness.

Living on Earth, however, I often find that people's ideas about happiness are very different from those of the inhabitants of the heavenly world. The majority of people think that happiness is something given to them by others and that the happiness they currently enjoy is in danger of being obstructed by

others, or *is* actually obstructed by them to some
extent. This is amazing, because in the home of souls
you always share in the happiness of others as if it
were your own. This being the case, I often feel this
world is very different from the other world.

How did this difference come about? When I pon-
der this, certain scenes come to mind, scenes I always
see as I descend from the far distant world of the ninth
dimension through the eighth, seventh, sixth, fifth, and
fourth dimensions of the spirit world. These scenes
can be compared to what is seen going down in an ele-
vator in a high-rise building. From inside a glass ele-
vator, you can see the scenery outside changing with
each second you descend. What was far below gradually comes into view, then it passes. In the same way,
when you pass through a dimension, the ground you
could see from high above comes rapidly closer, then
after you have passed through that layer, a new world
unfolds. To explain it in another way, it is like looking
down into water, and seeing multi-layered worlds
unfolding beneath the surface.

As I pass through numerous worlds, descending
from the faraway worlds of higher dimensions to
Earth, I notice that those who live in the lower realms
seem increasingly to lose trust in one another. The
facial expressions of the inhabitants of the different

dimensional worlds change—while those living in the higher dimensions are peaceful, cheerful, and filled with joy, the further I descend, the grimmer the faces and the more reserved people seem to be, obviously distrustful of one another.

If I take a look at the earthly world, I notice that many people trust no one but themselves, the reason being that each soul inhabits a kind of fortress known as a physical body. People's main interest is to protect themselves from outside enemies, confining themselves to their physical body as their fort. This phenomenon is so very different from our true nature, apparent in the home of souls. It is as if someone in full armor with a spear in his hand were to appear at a dinner party. How would you feel if someone in full armor suddenly appeared among all those attired in beautiful dresses and suits? It would certainly be strange. In the eyes of the angels in heaven, this earthly world looks just as unnatural.

2. Old Dear Friends

Looking deep into my heart, I remember the faces of my old friends in the home of souls. A great number of them now support me while I am here on Earth, either directly or indirectly, giving me spiritual messages. They are my old dear friends and my brother souls.

In the spirit world, I never felt that my power was limited; mostly my thoughts manifested instantly. In this world, however, it is difficult to accomplish things. As you face many different kinds of obstacles in real life and experience the difficulty of fulfilling your intentions, you may feel that your soul is gradually shrinking.

Why does the soul feel constrained, becoming small and shrunken on Earth? Pondering this question, I have found the reason. It is closely connected to the window of the heart. Everyone has a window in their heart; however, in those living on Earth the window of the heart is not open. Rather, it seems as if everyone is trying hard to keep it closed and not to show others what is inside.

If each person were to live with the heart open, as if it were transparent as glass, and no one felt uncomfortable with this, everyone would live in harmony. If people saw someone had a problem, they would rush to support and help that person. This is what actually happens in the spirit world. In this earthly world, however, people tend to hide what is on their minds from others and it is difficult to see into the mind of another. This world is full of people who do not try to understand one another's thoughts unless they are truly close.

My old friends in the spirit world are unguarded and their hearts are open; we understood each other's thoughts easily and there was no problem with that. We knew we would never hurt one another if we let each other know what we were thinking; rather, we became filled with the willingness to give others what they needed as soon as we knew their thoughts. As I recall the world of my old friends, I wonder why life on Earth is so difficult.

One reason for this difficulty is to be found in economic principles. Everything, even when connected with the manifestation of goodness, is subject to the economic principles that govern this world. While anything can be manifested instantly through the power of will in the spirit world, in this world nothing can be manifested unless you follow specific procedures that conform to economic rules, which require a lot of work from a number of people. You need to produce financial value, and to this end you must work. Through work, people come to desire the ownership of private wealth, and so the possessions of individuals become more and more clearly separated.

Everything you possess is God-given, so essentially you must use what you have for a worthy purpose. However, individuals insist on their right to possession; this was not part of the original plan. Although we originally inhabited a world where each person was open and willing to give, in this world we are surrounded by people who insist on their own rights, which gives rise to all sorts of suffering of the soul. Nevertheless, this world is still in the process of development and so this state of transition is unavoidable. For this reason, it is all the more important to consider how to bring this imperfect earthly life closer to the original state of the heavenly world.

3. Be Absolutely Truthful

It is true that we live in a world in which everyone insists on their own rights; some are even afraid that they may be deprived of their rights if they do not protect them vigorously. In the business world, people compete with one another to be outstanding. Those who study and convey the Truth are also bound by financial limitation. I cannot hold back my tears when I see them suffering financial hardship in every corner of the world. At the same time, I too am subject to the economic principles that rule this three-dimensional world, and I sometimes regret that I have to make a great deal of effort to create a financial basis for the further development of our Institute.

In the Real World, if something is truly in accordance with the will of God, it will manifest swiftly and many will gather round to support it. On Earth, however, even if we try to achieve something that accords with the will of God, we have to follow certain procedures to make it happen. This is a lot of work, but since these are the rules, or more accurately the system that our ancestors put in place on Earth, we must make all the more effort to keep our minds peaceful under these conditions and live as if we were in heaven.

Here I would like to offer one clue crucial to being able to live as if you were in heaven while leading a difficult life on Earth. If I were to summarize this in one phrase, it would be, "be intensely sincere." I would like you to lead an absolutely truthful life. On Earth, there are very few who truly live sincerely; people are too vain and use too many wiles. They are too quick to worry and take precautions against possible accidents. For example, when they meet someone, they are afraid of being deceived; when engaged in a business transaction, they worry they will be betrayed; they insure the life of their spouse from anxiety that if their partner dies they will be in trouble. In this way, distrust swirls through this earthly world. However, I hope that more and more people in this world will value the quality of sincerity. It is my wish that an increasing number of people will live honestly, and not feel embarrassed about revealing openly to others what is on their minds.

Ask yourself the following questions: Do you live in such a way that you would not be embarrassed if others were to read your mind all day long? Are you sure that you do not feel ashamed, knowing that God sees what is in your mind? Those who feel embarrassed have unharmonious thoughts; it is important to be pure, sincere, and truthful, without any vanity, like small children. To live with complete sincerity is an extremely difficult challenge in modern society, where there is so much confusion. However, unless many people determine to live in total sincerity, this world will not become a heavenly world. I cannot cease praying that more and more people will choose to believe and love others, instead of holding on to distrust.

4. The Path of Faith
I would now like to talk about the path of faith. In the past, I have not discussed faith much unless it was necessary, because I wanted everyone to discover the truth that lies in the depths of their own heart first, and to awaken to the inner voice of their conscience.

God exists and He gives us energy; He allows us to live. This means that essentially we should not spend a single day without thinking about God. In the past, however, I have not spoken much on this subject, because spiritual progress starts with correcting one's own mind. I believe that only when someone starts making an effort to correct their own mind do they have the right to look to God. Among those who pray to God are many hypocrites who do not have the will to correct their own minds, so I did not want to force people into this.

First, correct your own mind and explore the Right Mind for yourself. After the pursuit of the Right Mind, the path of faith will be open before you; you will be truly ready to face God, to discover the path to God, and to devote yourself to God. Exploration of the Right Mind does not mean living an egoistical life or denying the existence of angels or the transcendental consciousnesses of the spirit world. Rather, it is the effort to become qualified to walk on the path to God. Only when you have started to explore the Right Mind are you allowed to enter the path of faith.

The reason I have avoided discussing the subject of the path of faith is that people are still easily swayed by earthly vibrations, and the time has not yet come to talk about this. When those who study the Truth are able to maintain their minds at the same wavelength as the inhabitants of the heavenly world, and become able to live as if these inhabitants were actually living on Earth, then the order of the Real World will manifest naturally. The Real World is where people believe in one another and believe in God.

I hope that those who study the Truth will endeavor to manifest the true nature of the Real World and turn this three-dimensional world into a wonderful world of a higher dimension. Let us aim to create an ideal world, at the level of the seventh dimension, the Bodhisattva realm at least. Let us create a marvelous world where people live as altruistically as Bodhisattvas. Only when this has manifested will we be able to truly know God, and a path to God will open up before us. I believe that in trying to create a world of Bodhisattva on Earth through our own efforts, the path of faith that leads to God will unfold.

5. An Incomparably Pure Spirit

Lastly, I would like to discuss incomparably pure spirit. So far I have talked about the importance of the mind from a number of different angles. Perhaps some people confuse the mind with the spirit, so first I would like to define spirit.

Here, by spirit I mean a state of mind that accords with the will of God, a mind filled with noble ideals. There are many different states of mind, for example, the Right Mind, a beautiful mind, a virtuous mind, and a pious mind. I would call these states of mind that embody God's ideals "spirit." I want everyone to cultivate these states of mind. Rather than imagining the mind to be unstable like the waves of the ocean, I would like you to alter your concept of it to something with firm and sustaining foundations, attuned to high ideals.

There is no limit to the heights of spirit you can develop. No matter how much you purify your mind, it can never be enough, so it is important to continue to refine your character and develop a spirit that radiates light. Do not be controlled by emotions, but purify your mind and aim to achieve an incomparably high state.

What is "incomparably pure spirit"? It is the ultimate ideal human beings have long been seeking—the highest state of mind and the best possible way of living as an inhabitant of Earth. It is a state that future generations will hold up as an example to be followed, the state closest to the mind of God. Let us cultivate a highly purified spirit that will inspire others.

To this end, what do you need to do? First, remove the impurities from your mind every second of the day and, at the same time, think constantly about God. Do not forget to cultivate a state of complete devotion to

God, while continuing to purify your mind. It is important to accept your own smallness before God and yet have the continuous desire to fly high, to the home of souls. I hope you will continue to make an effort on a daily basis, aiming to cultivate "incomparably pure spirit."

Chapter Four

Ways to Get out of a Slump

1. Slumps in Life

I would like to talk about the slumps we sometimes experience in life. A slump is not merely a period when you have a lot of worries. While worries arise constantly out of individual circumstances, a slump is a low period within a larger life cycle. Someone who has gone through life without any significant problems might suddenly fall to a very low point in their life. When you are in a state of darkness like this, no matter how hard you try, nothing seems to work; you suffer and struggle, not knowing how to get out of your depression.

Everyone experiences a slump at some time in their life. Even those held to be experts on life are not immune. There might be a few people who go through life without encountering any major hardships, but for most of us this is not usually the case. A particular event may serve as the trigger that throws us into a kind of depression that we cannot get out of for some time.

There seem to be three major triggers for slumps. The first is a change in circumstances. If all the circumstances surrounding you have been too good, any change in them will automatically throw you into a slump. The second is a change in other people's opinion of you. The third is a little different from the other two. There seem to be cycles or tides of fortune that govern human lives and cause waves of good and bad events.

If you were to ask whether the theory of cycles in life is valid, the answer would be yes and no. Actually, in the Real World, there is a group of spiritual beings who research the tides of fate that govern human beings. They believe that certain cycles exist in human lives and that people should make plans and decisions according to these cycles. Usually they advise people on Earth not to make any important decisions or plan any major events during a period of depression. However, leading busy lives in the modern world, we cannot always afford to make decisions to do or not do things according to these cycles. We cannot ignore our everyday work routines; so even if there are certain cycles in life, we should not let them rule our lives. Are there really cycles that govern human beings, or is that a creation of the human mind? The truth is that although cycles do exist in human lives, they are not uniform or mathematical, nor do the same cycles apply to every individual. Life does not follow the same sequence for everyone; it is not like the order of the signs of the zodiac, which apply to everyone equally. Each person has his or her own particular cycles, which can be modified to a certain extent through effort.

Yet if you look back on your life so far, you will almost certainly notice ups and downs; lives without fluctuations are very rare. Actually, there is a purpose to the ups and downs in a life. In good times, you can savor happiness fully, and in bad times, your soul is strengthened through the process of overcoming pain and difficulties. For this reason you should not see a slump simply as negative but look at it from a deeper perspective.

2. The Causes of a Slump

What are the causes of a slump? Where can we find the direct triggers? As a person who knows the spiritual world, I do not intend to analyze slumps simply from a psychological point of view, because these low periods are often the result of spiritual factors. Taking these into consideration, I have discovered two main reasons why people fall into slumps. The first is that the soul needs rest. The second is that people tend to become pessimistic and sensitive to unhappiness as a result of negative spiritual influences.

Let us start by analyzing the first cause. You cannot continue to run at top speed all the time. At some point over a five- or ten-year period, even those who are generally successful in business sometimes experience a lack of energy, and become physically weak. At these times, people often become ill. A slump can be seen as the spiritual state preceding an illness or a physical breakdown; it is when the automatic control system of your soul is telling you that you are overheating. Just as the overheating of a car engine may precede an accident, the overheating of your soul may lead to a physical breakdown.

So you can see a slump as an indication that your soul is in need of rest. A spring cannot remain tightly wound forever; it fulfills its function only if it contracts and expands. Just as people generally need eight hours of sleep in a daily cycle, in longer cycles extending over five or ten or twenty years, you are at times forced to take periods of rest. This can be regarded as a matter of energy levels. Unless your "battery" has been charged sufficiently, you cannot give out power. If you continue to discharge energy, at some point you will need to recharge; and it is at such times you fall into a slump.

Now, let us look at the second cause. Although slumps occur as the result of negative spiritual influences, the direct cause of these slumps is to be found in events that occur in this material world. For example, when other people's opinions turn against you, or you experience a failure at work, you begin to worry and may become depressed for a certain period. In many cases, during this time you come under negative spiritual influences, and are affected by stray spirits.

You may think you need to take measures to counteract such influences, and, of course, if you are being affected by stray spirits you need to get rid of them. However, before you start thinking about doing this, I would like you to stop for a moment and look at the reason you have been affected. You need to be aware of why this has happened.

There is a set of laws that governs the spirit world, and stray spirits are only capable of affecting people on Earth within the scope of these laws. In other words, they cannot go against these laws to influence people. If they could, all the stray spirits would be able to escape from hell and possess the people on Earth; hell would become completely empty. However, the fact that it is not empty indicates that these spirits cannot come through into this world unless certain conditions are fulfilled.

What are these conditions? In fact, possession by these spirits is possible only when the wavelength of mind of a person on Earth is perfectly attuned to that of the spirit possessing him or her. In other words, the worries or interests of both parties must be exactly the same. Like the traditional Buddhist teaching, "one thought leads to three thousand worlds," you have the potential to attune to any realm of the spirit world with a single thought. It is as if everyone is constantly emitting thoughts like radio waves, and a person's frequency can be attuned to the frequency of certain stray spirits. So, when you are under the negative influences of these sorts of spirits, before blaming them entirely you need to reflect on your own state of mind.

3. The Lessons from a Slump

So far I have described what a slump is. What can you learn from these periods in your life? If you are in a depressed state, this is probably of some significance. At some point in your life, you will most likely encounter this sort of darkness, and you should not think of it as temporary or accidental but rather as something that occurs for a reason.

Let us consider the first set of circumstances in which you experience a slump as explained in the previous section—when you have exhausted your energy and you are spiritually weak. This happens when you have forgotten the Middle Way, a balanced way of living, something that I always teach is very important. Happiness is not to be found in extremes, and, if you wish to make progress, before you move forward you should first find the Middle Way.

Those who have burned out as a result of exhausting their energy should ask themselves if they have forgotten the Middle Way. For example, a man in a company may be judged unsuitable for a job and then dismissed from his position. One way of reacting to this situation is to see this as a sudden demotion and become depressed, but the problem may actually have started some time before. It is possible that this person did not have the ability to fulfill his responsibilities and may have been attempting to impress people by taking on more than he was really capable of.

It is very hard to assess one's own ability correctly. Ability consists of accumulated past experience and strength of character. If you lack experience and true strength of character but happen to be assigned to a demanding position supervising others, problems will naturally arise. If you try hard to continue fulfilling your responsibilities despite this, small troubles will gradually accumulate and eventually result in your failure. This happens because you have been unable to assess your abilities objectively and correctly.

In the international financial market, exchange rates fluctuate constantly according to economic conditions. In a sense, the value of people, too, fluctuates day to day, as if they also were subject to a system of fluctuating exchange rates. Successes add to your value and mistakes reduce it; on a smaller scale, your value rises and falls daily. In the same way as the rates of the yen, the dollar, and other currencies sometimes drop sharply, your rate may one day plummet. This may lead to a long period of depression, known as a slump.

However, this low period does not happen for no reason; so, if you find yourself in a depression, it is important to analyze all the possible reasons. Reflect deeply, for example, on the position you were in before the current slump and examine whether you really deserved it. You will probably find that you took it for granted or had forgotten how to be content, that you were concerned only with your own promotion or trying to attract the recognition of others. You may have become conceited and arrogant. I would like you to reflect on these points.

As for the second case, falling into a slump as a result of negative spiritual influences, the basic reason is the same. When you experience this sort of darkness, you are no longer able to attune to your guardian or guiding spirit. You need to contemplate deeply why you are unable to do this. The reason you cannot attune to your guardian spirit but instead have come under negative influences is often that in your mind you are excluding other people.

People who are in a slump are typically unwilling to do anything for others; they are often concerned only with themselves, just as people who are ill cannot think about anything other than their own physical condition. They need to be aware that, unwittingly, they have become self-centered. This being so, a slump teaches you a valuable lesson. It encourages you to understand the reason and the purpose for living. You need to be aware that because you have misunderstood this fundamental truth about life, you are in a state of depression.

4. Rising above Difficulties

How can we rise above difficulties or get out of a slump? I would like to look at this now. A period of depression is indeed painful. But if you are suffering in this way, it means that you must have been experiencing a time of glory before it. Had you lived quite ordinarily and never experienced glory, there would be no slump. A slump occurs in contrast to the brilliance of a time past, so, paradoxically, living an ordinary life might be a way to avoid slumps.

However, once we have been born into this world, we all aspire to realize our dreams. If the purpose of life is to endeavor to proceed toward high ideals, and if it is the will of the universe that we make an effort toward boundless progress, we should aim to achieve these goals. If we aspire to develop but find ourselves falling into a slump, what measures should we take to get out of it?

Firstly, I would like you to remember that you have an inexhaustible energy within. There is a source of infinite energy within you that wells up limitlessly. The soul is like an onion; in other words, it is a multi-layered structure, and the core is directly connected to God, the being who governs the entire universe. This central part of your soul is the source that provides you with boundless light.

What kind of power does this light have? In fact, this limitless light has the same power and attributes as God, which means it is filled with wisdom, justice, courage, compassion, love, harmony, and prosperity. So when you find yourself in a difficult situation, above all you should remember your true self. Be aware that essentially you have unlimited power. This awakening is the driving force that allows you to exercise limitless power within. Usually you put a lid on this limitless power of your soul. Although your true power is essentially infinite, welling up constantly like a mountain spring, unknowingly you stopper this spring with blind human thought. So it is very important always to be conscious of the source of this inexhaustible energy buried deep within you.

The second point is that I would like you to remember to concentrate on accumulation. A slump is a period when you have released so much energy that you do not have much left. At these times, you need to make an effort to build strength. In times of worry I always tell myself to concentrate on study. In the course of a long life, everyone experiences periods of worry, and at such times the wisest way of living is to focus on accumulating inner strength. A slump is sure to come to an end before too long, so take advantage of it by building up as much strength as possible.

The third important attitude is to see a setback as an opportunity to take time to think about other people's happiness. In a slump, people tend to think too much about themselves and forget about the others. So during this time, make an effort to change the object of your attention; think about how to make others happier.

It is not an overstatement to say that the best way to overcome a slump is to try to bring joy to others. Although you may be suffering, never try to vent your pain on others, or you will eventually cause yourself even more pain. If you are suffering, why not try to bring others joy? Because your own heart is filled with pain and sadness, it is all the more important to try to smile at others. At least you can try to make other people happier. Even when you are not happy in your present circumstances, resolve to discover the art of happiness and bring others joy, because people are always wishing for happiness. In walking this path, you will surely rise above this painful times.

5. Live with Great Poise

As I describe various ways of overcoming a slump, the image of an iceberg comes constantly to mind. As I have explained in *An Unshakable Mind*,[1] when you try to develop the stability of an iceberg, your depression will vanish of its own accord. The shape of an iceberg

---

1. Refer to *An Unshakable Mind* by Ryuho Okawa (Lantern Books, 2003), Chapter One: The Iceberg of Life.

illustrates the importance of having an accumulation of experience and inner strength. The part of an iceberg that can be seen above the surface of the water represents only one or two percent of the whole; the rest of the huge mass remains beneath the sea, providing stability.

Look again at the suffering and difficulties you encounter in the course of your life. No matter how difficult they may seem, the problems you encounter are equivalent to your problem-solving capacity. You will never be dealt problems that exceed your capacity to handle them. In other words, you will be given only as much hardship as your soul can cope with, never more. So do not waste too much time worrying; instead, concentrate on accumulating inner strength, developing the part beneath the surface that is unseen so that you will not to be swayed by any winds or storms, rain or snow.

I would like to suggest two important points for leading your life with stability and poise. First, aim to develop an unshakable mind, based on a firm aspiration to attain infinitely high ideals. An unshakable mind develops with ideals as its foundation. So set high ideals as a firm goal, and resolve to advance steadily, day by day.

Secondly, always aim to maintain serenity within. A calm, peaceful mind that is like the tranquil surface of a lake will stabilize you and give you balance against the winds and waves of life's difficulties. Try to build this serenity within, even as you lead a busy life. Unless you know this tranquil state of mind, you will not be able to withstand the storms of life. When you endeavor to make this world brighter, with a strong light that shines brilliantly from within, with an unshakable mind and inner serenity as your base, I have no doubt that a slump will have no choice but to melt away, like frost in the sunlight.

Chapter Five

Making Time Transparent

1. A Wonderful Life

Early summer is a beautiful time of the year. In this season of fragrant breezes, what do you think about? At this time of year I always think how wonderful life is because this is when green leaves are at their most beautiful. As summer approaches, the yellowish-green leaves become darker and darker and I feel my soul make dramatic progress, taking great strides forward.

These light green leaves of early summer express well a wonderful life. Just before nature experiences its full glory and all life is about to burst into bloom, we sense the vigor in the buds. I would like everyone to lead a life that is as beautiful as these light green leaves of early summer.

What constitutes a wonderful life? To be able to say that your life is magnificent, three conditions must be fulfilled. Firstly, your life must be unique and unparalleled. Secondly, you yourself must be able to declare that your life is glorious. Thirdly, you must have made great spiritual progress in this lifetime. There are, of course, other aspects to be considered when discussing a life that is glorious. In the past, I have often talked about the importance of perseverance, patiently building foundations on which to base your thoughts and behavior, and the importance of strengthening the inner self. But now, I would like to emphasize the importance of aiming for continual progress and becoming more and more active, exerting all of your energy.

In life, there are specific cycles like the four seasons in a year, and it is in the interval between spring and summer that you need to develop your abilities in areas where you have great potential. Otherwise, when are you going to develop your strengths? There is no better time than this. This is the time when I would particularly like you to study the philosophies that emphasize the bright side of life, such as positive thinking and the philosophy of progress, among the many ideologies I have introduced. I would like you to take this opportunity to make progress in your life and produce significant results.

What do you value most in life, and how are you going to develop this? In what direction do you want to set goals? Do you have any concrete plans? How much effort have you made and how many ideas have you come up with to achieve your goals? These are questions you need to find answers to. I sincerely hope that you will aim to make further progress in early summer.

2. Times of Enthusiasm

I have long pondered the meaning of time and have come to the conclusion that time is not something that exists outside of the human sphere; rather, it exists close to us, to the extent that we value it. Just like a pet dog or cat, the more we care for it and the better we treat it the better it seems to respond to us. When I am fired with enthusiasm, I feel time also heats up.

It is easy enough to imagine molten steel or a sword that is being tempered, but have you ever thought of time burning? Can you imagine time, which is usually invisible and transparent, becoming orange, gradually burning to a deep red? When your soul is full of energy and active, time becomes incandescent; you are excited to be doing something. This is when your soul is constantly moving forward, never stopping in its progress, striving for greater success.

This year, how often and for how long have you experienced time burning? If you say you have not experienced times of such excitement and have not felt that heat even once, now is the time to experience this. Year after year, you have three hundred and sixty-five days. If they just pass, and you are not on fire with enthusiasm for even a single moment, what is the point of living? Do you think you will feel satisfied if your heart is not on fire? Do you want to experience the burning of time? What do you want to put your heart into? What areas are you going to direct your passion into?

Now, before my eyes, a very vivid scene is unfolding, a future that radiates a brilliant light. It is my happiest vision, our Institute becoming more and more active, and the light of Truth gradually beginning to shine in every corner of the world. It is the most exciting mission, to do fulfilling work that goes hand in hand with happiness. The harder I work, the greater the number of people filled with joy and happiness, ensuring inexhaustible wonder and joy. I hope that everyone will feel the breath of this baking hot wind, and so step forward to convey the Truth with an inner enthusiasm, like the glow of a firefly.

There is no limit, no end to the mission of bringing happiness to the whole of humanity. So become more and more enthusiastic; live with your heart aflame so that time becomes incandescent. At least once a day, I would like you to be ablaze with enthusiasm. It is my sincere wish that you experience moments when you feel your palms become hot, your cheeks turn red, and joy fill your entire body.

These times are actually when you are attuned to the will of God and able to share happiness with others. If you are able to use your time to bring joy to others, this will be returned to you as a time of enthusiasm. I would like you to have many experiences of this kind.

3. Live Selflessly
In the last section, I recommended experiencing times of enthusiasm, living with passion and your heart on fire. When you are aflame with enthusiasm, I would like you also to live selflessly, like the fresh breezes of early summer.

Looking back through human history, there have been times when the torch of Truth was lit and its influence carried far and wide. On each occasion, there were leaders who worked hard to open up a new era and, when I think about the lives of these people, I see how selfless they were. They were ablaze with enthusiasm, but not like magma that burns up every-thing around it; rather, they lived in a selfless way.

How can you attain the quality of selflessness? To live selflessly, there are three requirements. The first is to have the courage to accept reality. In modern socie-ty, this seems to have lost its value long ago. People tend to worry about things that happened in the past and cling to them, unable to forget; in other words, they tend to become more and more obsessive. But when I think about someone who has the freshness of a breeze in early summer, he or she has the courage to accept reality as it is.

What exactly does it mean, to have the courage to accept reality? What is the refreshing quality that goes with bravery? I would like you to think about this. It actually means that while living passionately to achieve some grand purpose, you take responsibility and accept the outcome, be it success or failure. In other words, it means that you never make excuses. You devote all your efforts to achieving high ideals and, at the same time, you are not attached to the results. If you saw others living in this way, you would probably burst into hearty applause.

The second requirement is to share your happiness with others without expecting anything in return, instead of keeping your happiness to yourself. It is like a baker throwing freshly baked bread into the baskets of every passer-by, like a fresh wind. Imagine how pleasant it would be to live in this way. While people were walking happily to a picnic, carrying baskets in their hands, you would come up to them from behind, like a fresh breeze. As you passed, you would put freshly baked bread into each basket without their noticing. This is a nice way of giving love; giving love lightheartedly, without people even noticing. You might expect others to be aware of the love you are giving, but even if they do not notice you can still discover joy in the very act of continuous giving.

The third requirement for being able to say you are living selflessly is to understand that your life is finite and, at the same time, that it is eternal. If you see your life as finite, it means that you have only a certain number of years left on Earth. The amount of time left differs from person to person; for some, it may be five years, for some ten, others may still have twenty years to go. However, be it five, ten, or twenty years, it is important to accept the limited span of your life and think about how best to use your remaining years. By thinking in this way, you will feel much more lighthearted. Another aspect of this is that life is eternal. Even if you cannot achieve satisfactory results in this lifetime, since you have eternal life, you will be able to start over again in another lifetime.

To be able to live a selfless life, it is very important to have these two perspectives of time as both finite and infinite and use them accordingly. Sometimes see life as finite, and within this fixed amount of time make the utmost effort to find the most fruitful way of living. Then, on another occasion, know that your life is eternal and remain confident and stable like an enormous unsinkable ship on the Pacific Ocean. To be able to live with a selfless heart, it is important to use both these perspectives, of time as finite and infinite, depending on the situation.

4. Adopt a Wider Perspective

Another important aspect of living is to adopt a wider perspective. Those who are regarded as experts on living or whose knowledge is wide-ranging can view life from a wider perspective. When you are in difficulty, your mind is constantly swayed, and one way to get through this is to adopt a wider perspective. Try to view things with a higher awareness or from a completely different perspective, imagining yourself to be one of the great figures in history. When you are lost at the foot of a mountain, it is necessary to imagine how you would appear to someone at the top of the mountain.

However, living in a jungle of buildings, people in modern times know very little about what is outside. I would like them to go out of this jungle to broaden their views. However, if this is not possible, they at least need to try to visualize the whole sweep of the jungle from afar, from a great altitude. To put it another way, it is important to transcend the place that governs and restricts your present lifestyle. It is advisable to step out of your usual living space sometimes, for instance, out of your home, your workplace, or other places where you spend your time, and see yourself from the viewpoint of someone else.

I would hope that you are able to transcend time as well. Get rid of the perspective of this age, the perspective of a person living in the twenty-first century. Imagine how you would appear to someone living in the thirtieth century, or someone from the first century AD. This is one example of taking a wider-ranging view. It is important to have a perspective that transcends both time and space. In the eyes of others, people who view things in this way may seem quite dispassionate, but living this way is of great value.

5. Making Time Transparent

I have discussed many subjects. However, I would like to suggest a way of living in which time becomes transparent, like the winds of early summer. In the teachings of self-reflection, I emphasize the importance of removing attachments. This is not merely an old-fashioned idea belonging to ancient Buddhism; rather, the attitude of trying to free yourself from attachments is of great value to those who live in this present age.

What is an ideal way to live in modern times? The ideal is a passionate life and, at the same time, a selfless life; while you value the point of view of the present, you also transcend it. While concerned with the present, you are simultaneously detached from it. While constantly keeping your eyes on what is most important to you, you also give your attention to other matters. While putting all your energy into living in the present, you are also conscious of the past and the future. While you live with energy and passion, at the same time you are indifferent to and detached from the outcome. In this way, you are able to lead a selfless life.

While continuing to live in modern society, you can still rid yourself of attachments and become free of worldly desires. I sincerely hope that you will experience this way of living—when time becomes crystal clear, pure and transparent.

Chapter Six

Life and Originality

1. Freedom and Originality

In this chapter entitled "Life and Originality," I would like to introduce yet another perspective for improving life. I never stop thinking about this theme and, for several decades, I have been pondering the true meaning of originality.

Having been given human life in this world, if we can live in a way that is uniquely individual we will feel all the more joy. Human beings are children of God who have their origins in Him, but this does not mean that everyone looks the same or leads the same sort of life. Although we have the same essential nature, we are endowed with individuality and our unique flower is expected to bloom in its chosen place and time, in a specific environment on Earth.

The fact that human beings are children of God does not mean that we should lose our individuality and become identical. It does not mean that all flowers look exactly the same; rather, it means they have the same nature which encourages them to grow upward. The nature of the children of God is similar to the nature of flowers; although they all have the same nature, always seeking the sun and growing upwards, the way they grow, the way they blossom, and their colors are different. Flowers are equal in that they are all always trying to grow taller, but each one is assured the freedom to exert its individuality.

This being so, it is important to consider the idea of freedom, because it is closely connected to originality. How is freedom related to originality? I have discovered three main points in connection with this. First, freedom endows human beings with the energy for limitless growth. The freedom granted to human beings is a freedom that allows us to grow infinitely, a freedom that never leads us to degrade ourselves, or harm or annoy others. This infinite growth is closely related to the idea of originality, because seeking originality means trying to discover what has not yet been invented or developed, and once you have found it, trying to protect and nurture it. Originality includes growth, and this is closely connected to the idea of freedom.

2. A Predisposition to Goodness

The second point that I would like to talk about concerning the relationship between originality and freedom is the predisposition to goodness inherent in freedom. No matter how much originality you express, if your ideas are based on wrong thoughts they are not worthy of being called "original," because originality in the truest sense is very closely connected to the freedom to create that God possesses.

When God created the universe through exercising His freedom of creation, there was nothing to imitate. He created the universe out of nothing—this shows that God exercised His originality. His ideas were not only original but also oriented to goodness, and based on the wish for all beings to embody infinite goodness. If, for instance, God were mean and had intended to bully human beings, He could have established different kinds of spiteful mechanisms in this world. However, the reality is not like that; flowers blossom, birds fly, animals live without starving, and more than six million people are allowed to live different lifestyles. We are given sunlight, water, food, and especially life; we are allowed to live. At the basis of this world lies goodness, or the energy of goodness. It is obvious that when He created the universe, God had good intentions.

So when you are exercising your freedom, it is essential that you choose goodness, and aim to achieve goodness. In this sense, originality in life should be pursued from a perspective of serving the best interests of others as well as yourself. Otherwise, you cannot express originality in the truest sense. Originality without goodness leads only to satisfying your own interests and in the end, you will find yourself alone and miserable.

3. Love That Gives Infinitely

The third point I must mention in discussing freedom and originality is that originality is an expression of love. Expressing originality is one form of love, because creative ideas help many people to experience great benefits continuously, bringing them boundless prosperity. Take, for example, music. A masterpiece enriches human hearts all over the world, not only in the lifetime of the composer but also in future generations.

Another example is an excellent philosophy, which is of inestimable worth. The thoughts of the great figures of the past illuminate the darkness of human history through past, present, and future like lighthouses. A lighthouse casts light not only in front of a ship, but also behind, after it has passed by. In the same way, great figures of the past light up our path from behind and those of great stature in present times illumine our path ahead.

Can you imagine how many people have benefited from original philosophies that have ensured our safe passage through life? In many books I have described heaven and hell, and reading these descriptions some people may become fearful of the existence of hell and wonder why God allows such a terrible world to exist. If God expected us to sail across a pitch-black sea, that would indeed be merciless. However, the reality is that He built "lighthouses" everywhere and created the North Star, which always shines. We are given these through His compassion, and we are expected to advance safely on the journey of life with the help of the light from lighthouses and from the North Star. God has already given human beings guidance. He tells us to make our own efforts to live life to the fullest, following the guidance He provides. This shows the greatness of His love.

It is similar to the feelings of parents who take their small children to a pool to teach them to swim. To a child, who is still small and weak, the pressure of the water may be quite strong. However, if the parents walk through the water carrying the child on their back, or swim with the child in their arms, that will not be so good for the child. Although parents will sometimes extend a guiding hand, it is only natural that they want their children to swim by themselves, and to feel the joy of swimming. Parents want their children to experience the happiness of achieving their own goals. In life too, an outcome may seem to result in either happiness or unhappiness, but the fact that we have been endowed with freedom is in itself quite wonderful. It is clear that the basis of this freedom is love, not simply love that gives, but love that gives continuously and without any limits.

I have discussed originality in relation to freedom. To sum up, what I mean by originality is a source of love that encourages people to have as their aim a boundless growth toward goodness. Now perhaps you understand that true originality is far from egotistical.

In the world there are many artists who have the potential to be successful, and are active in an effort to develop their uniqueness. However, very few of them actually manage to create work that lasts for centuries or becomes internationally known. This is because most of them seek originality within the range of their personal tastes, or are constantly concerned about winning the admiration of others. Originality in the truest sense tends to reach beyond the self. True creative work leaves the hands of the person who produces it to enrich others, providing them with hope and dreams. This is the effect of true originality; it should not be confined to you, the creator, alone, as if you had patented it.

I have presented my thoughts in many different writings, and all of them have some degree of originality. However, I do not consider them my own personal belongings. The philosophy I teach will be more and more imitated, studied, and conveyed to many, and I believe that what is truly original will be studied and passed down to become the common treasure of all humanity.

4. A Sacred Time of Silence

Now I would like to introduce a concrete method for achieving originality in life. If your goal is to be creative in the course of your life, what do you need to do? Originality means one person creating something on their own. In the very word is hidden the meaning of a person continuing to think in complete solitude. Creating something in a sense implies a struggle with solitude. Those who exercise true originality spend quality time alone.

f solitude is necessary to ferment accumu-
...wledge and experiences through contempla-
tion, and to transform them into something completely new as if through a chemical reaction. In chemistry
classes, you may have conducted an experiment where
a transparent liquid suddenly turns red as you keep
adding a certain chemical. In the same way, if you continue to make an effort in solitude, your efforts will
change into something different when a certain critical
mass is reached. This is how a once-leaden life can be
turned into a shining, golden life; this is called the
alchemy of living.

I will now let you into the secrets of developing
creativity. There are three requirements to be fulfilled.
First, you need to wish sincerely to be useful, to be
someone who can contribute to society. Without this
intention, originality will never be born. Here lies the
difference between originality and the play of a young
child. It is important to have a strong wish to be of
service to the world and to benefit others. It is true that
the stronger this desire, the higher a person's spiritual
awareness; so blessed are those who have this powerful desire.

Secondly, you should never have the petty wish to
achieve only the selfish goals you hold at the moment.
It is important to wish to give something to those who

are younger, to future generations. If your aim is merely to be rewarded for your own efforts, there is nothing remarkable in this attitude. However, if you wish your efforts to be carried on by those who follow, without expecting any reward, this in itself is an inspiring attitude that goes beyond earthly concerns. I would like you to be determined to make an effort so that you can lead others to happiness, especially those who will be born in the future.

Thirdly, to change a leaden life to a golden one, a sacred time of silence is essential. People are always quiet in the moments just before they are about to create something. I would like you to know that it is in complete silence that the wisdom of humanity is born. So if you want to be creative, make an effort to take the time to remain silent. Through this process, a moment will come when your soul is suddenly changed.

I have given you three pieces of advice about becoming creative. It is my sincere wish that you will lead a brilliant life, a life abundant with originality. Instead of just leaving these ideas in your mind, please put them into practice and try to become creative, no matter how small your initial attempt. This is the moment when you, a caterpillar, will be transformed into a butterfly.

Postscript

In this book, I particularly wanted to address the importance of giving deep and serious consideration to the problems of the human mind. My real intention is to prompt each and every one of you to think about these issues, not only in an objective fashion, but as personal challenges.

No matter how many messages I write, no matter how many lectures I give, or how many books I publish on the theme of the human mind, people rarely see these problems as their own. In order for people to understand that these problems concern them directly, what is written needs to point to the truth, a truth that touches the heart and startles deep within.

This book contains descriptions that will surely touch the depths of your heart. If you feel pain, it is nothing less than a sign that you are now facing a challenge. Instead of trying to avoid this pain, I would like you to accept it calmly. Discover the diseased parts spreading through your mind and cut them out, then devote yourself to curing your disease completely. It is my heartfelt prayer that everyone will recover fully from the disease called unhappiness to lead a life of happiness.

Ryuho Okawa
President
The Institute for Research in Human Happiness

ABOUT THE AUTHOR

Ryuho Okawa, founder and spiritual leader of the Institute for Research in Human Happiness (IRH), has devoted his life to the exploration of the spirit world and ways to human happiness.

He was born in 1956 in Tokushima, Japan. After graduating from the University of Tokyo, he joined a major Tokyo based trading house and studied international finance at the Graduate Center of the City University of New York. In 1986, he renounced his business career and established IRH.

He has been designing IRH spiritual workshops for people from all walks of life, from teenagers to business executives. He is known for his wisdom, compassion and commitment to educating people to think and act in spiritual and religious ways.

The members of IRH follow the path he teaches, ministering to people who need help by spreading his teachings.

He is the author of many books and periodicals, including *The Laws of the Sun, The Golden Laws, The*

Laws of Eternity, *The Essence of Buddha*, *The Starting Point of Happiness* and *Love, Nurture, and Forgive.* He has also produced successful feature length films (including animations) based on his works.

What Is IRH?

The Institute for Research in Human Happiness (IRH), Kofuku-no-Kagaku in Japanese, is an organization of people who aim to refine their souls and deepen their wisdom. IRH spreads the light of the Truth, with the aim of creating utopia, an ideal world on Earth.

The teachings of IRH are based on the spirit of Buddhism. The two main pillars are the attainment of spiritual wisdom and the practice of love that gives.

Members study Buddha's Truth (the Law) and practice self-reflection daily, based on the Truth they learn. In this way they develop a deeper understanding of life and build qualities of leadership for society, enabling them to contribute to the development of the world.

Self-Development Programs

Video lectures and meditation seminars are held at each branch office. By attending seminars, you will be able to:

- Know the purpose of life.
- Know the true meaning of love.
- Know the Laws of success.
- Learn to understand the workings of your soul.

- Learn the importance of meditation and methods.
- Learn how to maintain peace of mind.
- Learn how to overcome the challenges in life.
- Learn how to create a bright future, and more…

IRH MONTHLY MESSAGES

This features lectures by Ryuho Okawa. Each issue also includes a question and answer session on real life problems with Ryuho Okawa. Anyone is able to subscribe to the IRH Monthly Messages. Back issues are also available upon request.

MEDITATION RETREAT

Educational opportunities are provided for people who wish to seek the path of Truth. The Institute organizes meditation retreats for English speakers in Japan. You will be able to find keys to solve the problems in life and restore peace of mind.

For more information, please contact our branch offices or your local area contact.

THE INSTITUTE FOR RESEARCH
IN HUMAN HAPPINESS
Kofuku-no-Kagaku

Tokyo
1-2-38 Higashi Gotanda
Shinagawa-ku
Tokyo 141-0022
Japan
Tel: 81-3-5793-1729
Fax: 81-3-5793-1739
Email: tokyo@irh-intl.org
www.irhpress.co.jp

New York
Suite 58
725 River Road
Edgewater, NJ 07020
Tel: 1-201-313-0127
Fax: 1-201-313-0120
Email: ny@irh-intl.org

Los Angeles
Suite 104
3848 Carson Street
Torrance, CA 90503
U.S.A.
Tel: 1-310-543-9887
Fax: 1-310-543-9447
Email: la@irh-intl.org

San Francisco
1291 5th Ave.
Belmont, CA 94002
U.S.A.
Tel / Fax: 1-650-802-9873
Email: sf@irh-intl.org

Hawaii
Suite 19
1259 South Beretania Street
Honolulu, HI 96814
U.S.A.
Tel: 1-808-591-9772
Fax: 1-808-591-9776
Email: hi@irh-intl.org

Toronto
484 Ravineview Way
Oakville, Ontario L6H 6S8
Canada
Tel: 1-905-257-3677
Fax: 1-905-257-2006
Email: toronto@irh-intl.org

London
Room T, 2nd Floor
Warwick House
181/183 Warwick Road
London W14 8PU
United Kingdom
Tel : 44-20-7244-6199
Fax: 44-20-7244-7648
Email: eu@irh-intl.org

Sao Paulo
(Ciencia da Felicidade do
Brasil)
Rua Gandavo
363 Vila Mariana
Sao Paulo, CEP 04023-001
Brazil
Tel: 55-11-5574-0054
Fax: 55-11-5574-8164
Email: sp@irh-intl.org

Seoul
178-6 Songbuk-Dong
Songbuk-ku, Seoul
Korea
Tel: 82-2-762-1384
Fax: 82-2-762-4438
Email: korea@irh-intl.org

Melbourne
P.O.Box 429 Elsternwick
VIC 3185
Australia
Tel / Fax: 61-3-9503-0170
Email: mel@irh-intl.org

Taiwan
5F, No.109-7
Hsin yi Road, Section 3
Taipei, Taiwan
Tel: 886-2-2705-8097
Fax: 886-2-2705-8302
Email: taiwan@irh-intl.org

**OTHER E-MAIL
CONTACTS**

Florida
Email: florida@irh-intl.org

Albuquerque
Email: abq@irh-intl.org

Boston
Email: boston@irh-intl.org

Chicago
Email:chicago@irh-intl.org

Hong Kong
Email: hongkong@irh-intl.org

Other Asian Countries
Email: asia@irh-intl.org

Lantern Books by Ryuho Okawa

The Laws of the Sun
The Spiritual Laws & History Governing Past,
Present & Future
1-930051-62-X
Lantern Books, 2001

The Golden Laws
History through the Eyes of the Eternal Buddha
1-930051-61-1
Lantern Books, 2002

The Laws of Eternity
Unfolding the Secrets of the
Multidimensional Universe
1-930051-63-8
Lantern Books, 2001

The Starting Point of Happiness
A Practical and Intuitive Guide to Discovering Love,
Wisdom, and Faith
1-930051-18-2
Lantern Books, 2001

Love, Nurture, and Forgive
A Handbook to Add a New Richness to Your Life
1-930051-78-6
Lantern Books, 2002

An Unshakable Mind
How to Overcome Life's Difficulties
1-930051-77-8
Lantern Books, 2003

The Origin of Love
On the Beauty of Compassion
1-59056-052-3
Lantern Books, 2003

Invincible Thinking
There Is No Such Thing As Defeat
1-59056-051-5
Lantern Books, 2003

Want to know more?

Thank you for choosing this book. If you would like to receive further information about titles by Ryuho Okawa, please send the following information either by fax, post or e-mail to your nearest IRH Branch.

1. Title Purchased

_____

2. Please let us know your impression of this book.

_____

3. Are you interested in receiving a catalog of Ryuho Okawa's books?

     Yes ❑   No ❑

4. Are you interested in receiving IRH Monthly?

     Yes ❑   No ❑

Name : Mr / Mrs / Ms / Miss : _____

Address : _____

_____

Phone: _____

Email: _____

Thank you for your interest in Lantern Books.

2/2/13.